SANATANA JYOTI

The Spiritual Journey of Kanchi Maha Periyava's Life Journey from 1894 to 1939

Vol 1

Vijay Vasudevan

INDIA · SINGAPORE · MALAYSIA

Contents

Contents

Contents

From the sacred soil of Villupuram to the banks of the Ganga, this book traces the divine journey of Kanchi Maha Periyava from His birth in 1894 to the culmination of His monumental Kashi Yatra in 1939. It is the story of a child born with the radiance of ancient wisdom, who rose to become the beacon of Sanatana Dharma. Through silence, austerity, and grace, Periyava walked across Bharat, reviving traditions, uplifting souls, and awakening a timeless spiritual consciousness. This is not just a biography—it is a pilgrimage through the early life of a living incarnation.

गुरु ब्रह्मा गुरु विष्णुः गुरु देवो महेश्वरः।
गुरु साक्षात् परब्रह्म तस्मै श्री गुरवे नमः॥

Meaning

The Guru is Brahma (the Creator), Vishnu (the Preserver), and Maheshwara (Shiva – the Destroyer).

The Guru is verily the embodiment of the Supreme Brahman. I bow down in deep reverence to such a Guru.

Maha Periyava – The Jagadguru, The Living Grace

O Holy Sage, **Jagadguru Sri Maha Periyava**, You are the very embodiment of compassion, wisdom, and divine grace. In you, we see the silence of Shiva, the discipline of Shankara, the knowledge of the Vedas, and the boundless love of a mother. You walked among us in silence and simplicity, yet carried within you the essence of the *Sanatana Dharma*, the power of penance, and the brilliance of true realization.

We bow to you, *O Paramaacharya*, who is not just the Guru for a few, but the **Guru of the world** – *Jagadguru*. Like Brahma, you created a resurgence of Dharma; like Vishnu, you protected traditions through your words and actions; and like Shiva, you dissolved ignorance with your mere gaze.

Your very presence sanctified the land, your silence was louder than a thousand discourses, and your glance carried the weight of universal wisdom. Even today, your footsteps echo in the temples, forests, rivers, and hearts of the devotees.

Sri Mahaswami pweforming anushtanam at Sandur - 1978

A Humble Prayer

We surrender at your lotus feet, O Jagadguru Maha Periyava. Bless us with wisdom to walk the path of righteousness. Give us strength to uphold Dharma in every step of life. Let our minds be free of ego, our hearts be filled with love and devotion, and our actions reflect your teachings.

Just as the sloka says, you are indeed *Guru Brahma, Guru Vishnu, Guru Devo Maheshwara* – But above all, you are **Guru Sakshat Parabrahma** – the living embodiment of the Supreme.

Tasmai Shri Gurave Namah – We bow eternally at your holy feet.

Brahmasri Ganesa Sarma

My Manaseega Guru

This book is a humble offering, inspired by the profound wisdom and captivating narration of Brahmasri Ganesa Sarma, whom I consider my Manaseega Guru. His enlightening discourses and deeply insightful explanations of Maha Periyava's journey have been my guiding light, shaping my understanding and reverence for this spiritual odyssey. Through his words, I have not only learned about the life and legacy of Maha Periyava but have also imbibed the essence of his teachings, which have motivated me to pen down this work.

The way Brahmasri Ganesa Sarma has brought to life the divine journey of Maha Periyava, illuminating the depths of his wisdom, austerity, and boundless compassion, has been a source of immense inspiration. With this book, I aspire to share that same reverence and devotion, offering a glimpse into the spiritual magnificence of Maha Periyava.

May this work serve as a tribute to both my Guru and the timeless legacy of Maha Periyava, whose grace continues to guide countless seekers on the path of dharma.

PREFACE

For the past 25 years, I have lived and worked in Mumbai, deeply immersed in the material world—chasing career aspirations and financial success. My life revolved around professional achievements, and I took great pride in my hard work and dedication. However, in August 2024, something within me began to shift. A profound transformation unfolded, one that I never saw coming. It is this personal journey that I wish to share, along with the inspiration behind this book.

Throughout my career, I steadily climbed the corporate ladder, believing that my success was solely the result of my relentless work ethic. But in the past year and a half, I began facing unexpected obstacles—interruptions and setbacks that arose not from my shortcomings but from the personal agendas of others. These challenges prompted me to step away from my organization, and soon, I started receiving multiple job offers.

Then, one morning, at around 4:30 AM, I had a dream that would change everything. In the dream, Kanchi Maha Periyava appeared before me and said, "Don't worry, I have told them. You come to Chennai and visit Kanchipuram." The dream ended abruptly, leaving me bewildered. Though I have always been a believer in God, I had never followed Maha Periyava. In fact, I had never visited Kanchipuram nor listened to any of his discourses.

That very same day, something extraordinary happened. I received an unexpected call from a bank in Chennai. The HR Head—an old acquaintance from my Tata days, with whom I hadn't spoken in years—reached out and said, "I believe you are looking for a change. We have a suitable opening here. Would you be interested?" I was stunned. Without hesitation, I said, "Yes, of course!" He then invited me for an interview.

The interview was scheduled for 2 PM, and I had booked a return flight to Mumbai for the same night at 8 PM. During the interview, I was informed of another round at 5:30 PM. Since I needed to leave by 5 PM for my flight, we decided to schedule the final round for the following week. Just as we were discussing this, I received a message from Indigo Airlines—my flight was delayed by two and a half hours, now departing at 10:30 PM. I immediately informed the HR team that I could attend the final round that very day.

On my way to the airport, I reflected on the series of events. Was this merely a coincidence? The flight delay happened at the exact moment when we were planning to postpone the interview. It felt as though Maha Periyava himself was orchestrating everything. What else could explain it?

Once I received my offer, I decided to drive from Mumbai to Chennai, planning to join the bank on September 16, 2024. The night before my journey, I couldn't sleep. Restless and awake, I finally set off at 5 AM. After several hours of driving, I reached Satara, where exhaustion overtook me. My eyes burned, and I was struggling to stay awake. Fear gripped me—I was too tired to continue but hesitant to stop. I considered booking a hotel room to rest but instead decided to pull over and nap in my car.

I called my wife and told her, "I will sleep for an hour in the car. If I still feel exhausted, I will check into a hotel." She was scared and urged me to return to Mumbai. But something within me pushed me forward. Before closing my eyes, I prayed, "Periyava, please guide me. Should I go back or continue to Chennai?"

Then, in that moment of half-sleep, I heard a clear voice say, "Have a coffee, refresh yourself, and drive." Startled, I opened my eyes. The voice was in Tamil, and I was completely alone in the car. Overwhelmed yet reassured, I stepped out, went to the nearby hotel, had a coffee, and washed my face. The exhaustion vanished. My eyes cleared, my mind felt fresh, and I was filled with newfound energy. I drove continuously without stopping for lunch and reached my hotel in Hubli by 5 PM.

How do I explain this experience?

From that day onward, Often Periyava talking to me and I have firmly feel his presence is always with me, guiding me at every step. I am certain that it is his divine will that has led me to write this book. *Hara Hara Shankara, Jaya Jaya Shankara!*

Since that moment, I have immersed myself in the discourses (Upanyasam) of Brahmasri Ganesa Sarma on Maha Periyava. This book is the mere outcome of his discourse.

This book is a humble offering—an attempt to weave a garland of devotion at the lotus feet of Maha Periyava.

By, Vijay Vasudevan

01

THE DIVINE CHILD

On a serene morning, on May 20, 1894, in the humble town of Villupuram, Tamil Nadu, a divine child was born to Sri Subramanya Sastri and Smt. Mahalakshmi Ammal. This child, named Swaminathan Sharma, arrived as the second son in the family, unaware that he was destined for a path that would change the spiritual fabric of India. No one could have foreseen that this boy would one day ascend as the 68th Shankaracharya of the Kanchi Kamakoti Peetham, known by the revered name of **Shri Chandrasekarendra Saraswathi Swamigal**. Devotees across the world would come to adore him as **Kanchi Maha Periyava, Mahaswami, Jagadguru, and The Sage of Kanchi.**

Swaminathan was born into a pious family with Five siblings—his elder brother, Ganapathi Sastri, and Four younger siblings named Sambamurthy, Lalithamba, Sadasivam (Later known as Sivan Saar) and Krishnamurthy (Kunju Sastri). Although the second child, Swaminathan held a special place in his parents' hearts due to his exceptional intelligence, wisdom, and innate spiritual inclination from an early age.

Photo: The Villupuram House where Maha Periyava Born on 1894

His father, Sri Subramanya Sastri, served as a teacher and later as a district education officer. His profession required the family to relocate frequently, exposing Swaminathan to different environments during his formative years. One such place was Tindivanam, a town in Tamil Nadu, where a momentous event in Swaminathan's spiritual journey unfolded.

Photo: Swaminathan (3rd from Let in first row) at Arcot American Mission School, Thindivanam - 1906

A Sacred Encounter

Upon reaching the appropriate age, Swaminathan underwent Upanayanam—a sacred thread ceremony that marks the formal initiation of a young Brahmin into the study of the Vedas and spiritual life. Following this rite of passage, he, along with his parents, visited the 66th Shankaracharya of the Kanchi Kamakoti Peetham, who was then residing in Perumukkal. It was during this visit that an extraordinary connection between the young boy and the revered saint was established.

As soon as Swaminathan set foot in the presence of the 66th Acharya, We can guess something profound transpired. Unlike the brief blessings offered to most visitors, the Acharya engaged in a long, deep conversation with the child. Those present in the monastery watched in awe as the Jagadguru and the little boy conversed for hours, as if reuniting after ages. The Acharya, sensing the divine spark in Swaminathan, turned to his father and instructed, "Bring

Swaminathan to the Mutt often." From that day on, forging a bond beyond the comprehension of ordinary mortals.

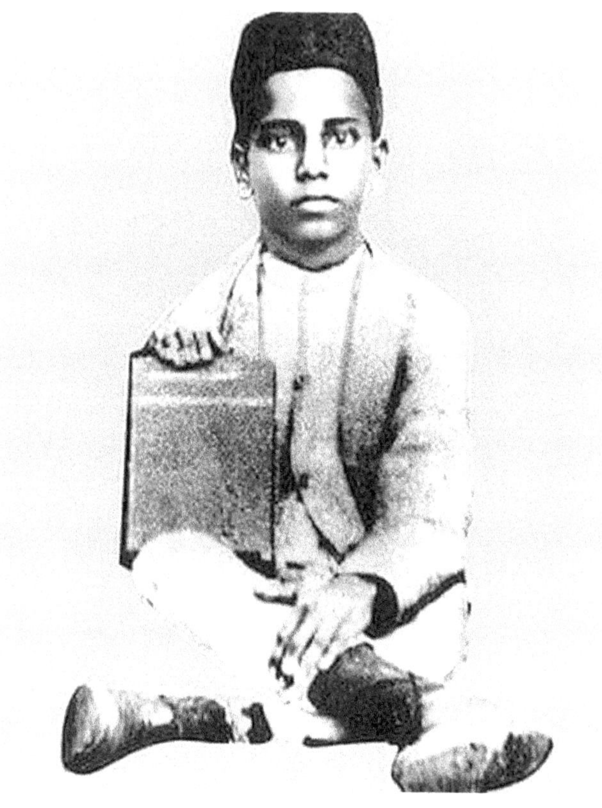

Photo: Sri Swaminathan in Purvaasramam – 1906 at School

The Call of the Guru

Some time later, the 66th Acharya moved from Perumukkal to Saaram as Chaturmasya period is over—a four-month spiritual retreat observed by monks. Though young, Swaminathan felt an inexplicable pull toward the Acharya, an urge so strong that it began occupying his thoughts day and night. He longed to meet his guru again.

One fine morning, before dawn, Swaminathan awoke during Brahma Muhurta, the sacred period of divine energy, and set out on a determined journey. First, he tried waking up his friend, Krishnaswamy, but the boy refused to rise at such an early hour. Undeterred, Swaminathan approached Ramakrishnan, Krishnaswamy's cousin, who agreed to accompany him.

Thus, two young boys, filled with devotion and innocence, embarked on an arduous journey, walking over 12 kilometres to Saaram, just to see the Acharya.

As the sun rose, their little feet ached from the relentless walk. The sweltering heat drained their energy, but Swaminathan's unwavering resolve to see his guru kept him going. As they walked, he recounted to Ramakrishnan the mesmerizing experience of meeting the Acharya before. Suddenly, they spotted a bullock cart making its way toward Saaram.

Divine Providence and a Test

Hopeful, Swaminathan and Ramakrishnan hurried toward the cart. "Mama, Mama!" Swaminathan called out. "We are going to see my Acharya at the Kanchi Mutt. Could you please give us a ride?"

The man sitting behind the cart was Karvar Venkatarama Iyer, an administrator of the Mutt, holding the esteemed position of Karvar, responsible for its overall management. Unknown to the children, the Acharya himself was traveling in a palanquin (Mena) ahead of the cart.

But Karvar Venkatarama Iyer was a strict disciplinarian. "This cart belongs to the Mutt," he sternly replied. "It cannot be used by outsiders."

His words crushed Swaminathan's hopes. His heart sank, but his spirit remained unshaken. He simply nodded, accepting the divine play of fate, and continued walking alongside the cart toward Saaram.

A Guru's Affection

When they finally reached Saaram, the Acharya stepped out of his palanquin and immediately spotted Swaminathan among the gathered devotees. A smile of recognition spread across his face. "Swaminatha! How did you get here? Where is your father?" he asked with affectionate surprise.

Swaminathan, beaming with devotion, replied, Periyava I wanted to meet you again, so I walked all the way."

The Acharya was deeply moved. He knew instantly that this boy was no ordinary soul—a connection from a past life had drawn them together once more. He instructed his attendants to take the children inside, give them water, and ensure they were well-fed.

Understanding the gravity of the situation—that a young boy had traveled far without his parents' knowledge—the Acharya immediately sent a messenger to inform Swaminathan's family that he was safe and would return in two days. However, there was a divine reason behind keeping Swaminathan with him for this short period—for the Acharya, a Trikala Jñāni (knower of past, present, and future), foresaw that Swaminathan will be the next Acharya for this peetam and in his absence.

The Revelation of Destiny

Back in Tindivanam, Swaminathan's parents were frantic upon discovering his absence. Panic spread through the household, and they searched the entire village in vain. Just as their despair peaked, a cart arrived at their doorstep with news from the Mutt. Relief washed over them upon learning that Swaminathan was safe, yet his father, Subramanya Sastri, was deeply troubled. What had possessed his young son to leave home without informing them?

Two days later, Swaminathan returned home in the very bullock cart that had once refused him a ride—an irony orchestrated by fate. The moment he stepped inside, his parents embraced him tightly, their eyes brimming with joy and concern. Yet, Subramanya Sastri could not shake off a nagging worry. What was Swaminathan's destiny? Was there a hidden divine plan at work?

Seeking answers, he approached a learned astrologer, Venkataramaiah, a close family friend. Upon reading the boy's horoscope, the astrologer fell silent, stunned. Tears welled in his eyes as he recognized the signs of an Avatara Purusha (divine incarnation).

Then Venkataramaiah said, "Subramanya! You please go and bring Swaminathan here. I want to see his palm and footprint reading." Subramanya Sastri went and brought Swaminathan.

Venkataramaiah asked Swaminathan to go and wash his feet in the backyard and come with some water in a small pot. Swaminathan did as instructed and brought a small pot of water. Venkataramaiah took Swaminathan's feet, washed them, wiped them with a towel, and placed them in his lap before starting to read the footprints.

Subramanya Sastri had no clue why this was happening, and the same was true for Swaminathan.

Venkataramaiah continued reading the footprints. Time passed, and he was stunned by what he saw. Tears started rolling from his eyes as he held both of Swaminathan's feet close to his chest for some time. Silence prevailed.

Swaminathan felt a bit uncomfortable with an elder holding his legs and stared at his father.

Subramanya Sastri said, "Hey Venkataramaiah! What is happening? Please tell me what you have seen. Is everything okay?"

Venkataramaiah replied, "Hey Subramanya! This is the time to touch and embrace these feet. People may queue up to touch these feet. I am so lucky to have them close to my heart."

Further, he explained what he had seen. "Subramanya! certain divine Rekhas (prints) like Shankha Rekha, Chakra Rekha, Dhanur Rekha, Padma Rekha, and Makara Rekha. I have seen in Swaminathan's foot. This is a miracle.

For example, if you buy Vishnu Padam from Gaya (Kashi), you will see these same Shankha, Chakra, Dhanur, Padma, and Makara Rekhas on them. So there is no doubt."

Venkataramaiah then said, **"Subramanya! Stop worrying. Your son is no ordinary child. His destiny is far beyond what we can comprehend."**

Thus, the first whispers of Swaminathan's divine mission were revealed—his path, already written in the stars, was unfolding before the world's eyes.

ॐ

02

The Divine Calling of Swaminathan

The Fateful Telegram

Days passed after their meeting with Venkataramaiah. One fine day, Subramania Sastri was away on an official visit to Tiruchirappalli when an urgent telegram arrived from Kanchi Mutt. At that time, the 66th Acharya of Kanchi Kamakoti Peetham was camped at Kalavai, a village approximately 40 kilometers from Kanchipuram.

The telegram came to Swaminathan's house addressing Subramanya Sastri to bring Swaminathan to Kalavai Mutt immediately.

In the meantime the 66th Acharya had contracted smallpox, a deadly disease in those days with little chance of survival. Realizing that his time was near, the Acharya, in his infinite wisdom, decided to choose his successor. He decided that **Swaminathan has to be brought to Kalavai immediately to receive Sannyasa and take over as the next Acharya of the Kanchi Kamakoti Mutt.**

This event alone showcases the **Trikala Jñānam** (knowledge of past, present, and future) of the 66th Acharya. He had foreseen Swaminathan's spiritual destiny when he first met him in Perumukkal and Saaram. The world would later witness how this young boy would go on to be revered as **Maha Periyava—the Walking God—for the next 83 years.**

The Dilemma of Mahalakshmi Amma

With Subramania Sastri away, the telegram was received by Mahalakshmi Amma, Swaminathan's mother. The sudden directive left her confused and anxious. In those days, women were neither accustomed to making decisions alone nor traveling without a male companion. She had no means to contact her husband and was left clueless about the true purpose behind the Acharya's request.

She faced a dilemma—how to take Swaminathan to Kalavai? What did the Acharya intend? The uncertainty weighed heavily on her.

An Unexpected Turn of Events

Meanwhile, the condition of the 66th Acharya worsened, and he attained Siddhi (left his mortal body). A Mutt cannot exist without a Peetadhipathi (spiritual head), so urgent steps were taken to appoint a successor. Since Swaminathan had not yet arrived, the Mutt decided to confer Sannyasa on Lakshmikanthan, Swaminathan's cousin, who had been serving the 66th Acharya with deep devotion. He was given the monastic name Sri Mahadevendra Saraswati Swamigal and became the 67th Acharya.

When Mahalakshmi Amma heard this news, she was deeply moved for the fate of her sister, whose only son had now become a Sannyasi. Her sister had already lost her husband, and now, she had to part with her son forever due to his monastic vows.

Still unaware of Swaminathan's divine calling, she believed the telegram was merely an invitation for Lakshmikanthan's coronation ceremony. Encouraged by the villagers, she took Swaminathan and his siblings and set out for Kanchipuram by train.

Divine Will Unfolds

However, destiny had a different plan.

Lakshmikanthan, having served the ailing 66th Acharya, also contracted smallpox. Within eight days of taking Sannyasa, he too attained Siddhi. Before passing, he realized the divine will and sent a messenger to Kanchipuram with instructions to bring Swaminathan to Kalavai to assume the Peetadhipathi's position.

At the same time, Mahalakshmi Amma and her children reached Kanchi Mutt, unaware of the unfolding events. The Mutt administrators, burdened with the heavy task of breaking the news to her, hesitated. They asked her to stay back in Kanchipuram and instructed Swaminathan to accompany the messenger to Kalavai.

The Journey to Kalavai

Swaminathan, still a 13 year old boy, was unaware of what lay ahead. He believed his cousin was the Acharya and assumed he was being sent to serve him. As he boarded the bullock cart, the messenger solemnly informed him:

"Swaminatha! You cannot return home from now. You will be in the Mutt forever."

These words struck the young boy like lightning. As the cart rumbled along the dusty path, realization dawned upon him. His cousin had also passed away, and he was being called to take Sannyasa. At just 13 years of age, he was about to be thrust into the highest spiritual seat of the great Kanchi Kamakoti Peetham.

The weight of this revelation was unbearable. Overwhelmed and speechless, Swaminathan buried his head between his knees and chanted "Rama Nama" continuously until he reached Kalavai.

श्री राम जय राम जय जय राम ॥
Shri Rama Jaya Rama Jaya Jaya Rama ॥

This mantra, widely propagated by Samarth Ramdas, the 17th-century saint and spiritual guide to Chhatrapati Shivaji Maharaj, became Swaminathan's source of strength and surrender.

The Parents' Agony

By this time, Subramania Sastri had returned to Thindivanam and learned of the shocking events. He rushed to Kanchipuram, and together with Mahalakshmi Amma, they hurried to Kalavai. There, they received the news that both the 66th and 67th Peetadhipathis had passed away, and Swaminathan was now chosen as the next Acharya.

The reality was overwhelming. Their young son, still in school, was to renounce the world forever. They were heartbroken—not only because they were losing their beloved child but also because they feared whether he would be able to bear the immense responsibility of leading a spiritual institution that had thrived for over 2500 years.

People consoled them, reassuring them of divine will. Yet, their parental instincts kept them anxious—how could a small boy handle such a monumental task?

Swaminathan's Unwavering Resolve

At that moment, it was not the elders but Swaminathan himself who gave them confidence.

With remarkable composure, he addressed his parents:

"Dear Appa and Amma, please do not worry. This decision was not made by me but by the great Acharyas of the Mutt. Their

decisions never fail. They will give me the power and wisdom to fulfill this duty. So, surrender yourself to Guru's will and do not grieve."

His words left everyone astounded. How could a mere child display such wisdom and detachment? His parents were moved to tears. They had lost their son to the world, but they had given him to the divine.

The Final Goodbye

That was the last time Subramania Sastri and Mahalakshmi Amma saw and spoke to their son. From that moment on, their child was no longer Swaminathan—he was now the Acharya of Kanchi Kamakoti Peetham.

The world would come to witness his unparalleled spiritual wisdom, his boundless compassion, and his extraordinary service to Sanatana Dharma. He would become revered as Kanchi Maha Periyava, the guiding light of countless devotees.

Yet, the parents who gave this divine treasure to the world could never see their child again. Such is the path of renunciation, where personal ties are sacrificed for the greater good of humanity.

This was not just the story of a young boy becoming a spiritual leader. **It was the unfolding of divine will, the play of destiny, and the manifestation of Guru's grace.**

From that day forward, **Sanatana Dharma had found its greatest beacon of light—Kanchi Maha Periyava, the eternal flame of wisdom and compassion.**

03

THE ASCENSION TO THE 68TH PEETADHIPATH

Maha Periyava's Pattabishekam and the Spiritual Reawakening of Kanchi Kamakoti Peetam

On February 13, 1907, a pivotal moment in spiritual history unfolded in Kalavai. Swaminathan, under the acceptance of Sri Subramanya Sastri and Smt Mahalakshmi Amma, was anointed the 68th Acharya of the revered Kanchi Kamakoti Peetam. He was named Sri Chandrasekharendra Saraswati and embraced the Sanyas Ashram. This event marked the beginning of a sacred journey that would leave an indelible impact on Indian spiritualism. However, the path ahead was not without its challenges.

Photo: Maha Periyava at Kalavai in 1907

A Call to Lead Amid Adversity

For Maha Periyava, this was a time of immense spiritual and emotional upheaval. Both his Guru and Parama Guru had attained

Siddhi, leaving him with the daunting responsibility of leading the Peetam. Despite the weight of these expectations, Periyava rose to the occasion, meticulously performing the rituals that accompanied the transition to the Peetadhipathi role.

After completing these vital rites, Maha Periyava made his way to Kumbakonam, where on May 7, 1907, his Pattabishekam as the 68th Peetadhipathi was performed at the Kumbakonam Mutt. The event was graced by the presence of many prominent figures, including the Maharaja of Tanjavur, government officials, and respected pundits, symbolizing the spiritual renaissance that was beginning under his guidance.

The Legacy of Adi Shankaracharya

The deep spiritual significance of Kanchi traces its roots to the legendary Adi Shankaracharya (509 BC), who established the Shankara Mutt in Kanchipuram as part of his mission to revive Sanatana Dharma and Advaita Vedanta. Shankaracharya's journeys across Bharata Varsha laid the foundation for the intellectual and spiritual renaissance of the subcontinent, and Kanchipuram became a central hub for this transformative movement.

Kanchipuram holds a revered position in the list of the Sapta Moksha Puris, the seven sacred cities believed to grant liberation. It is as spiritually significant as Kashi (Varanasi) for Shiva, Ayodhya for Rama, Mathura for Krishna, Ujjain for Mahakaleshwar, Haridwar for Vishnu, Dwarka for Krishna, and Avantika for Mahakala. It is home to the divine goddess Kamakshi and continues to be a major seat of Advaita Vedanta, as established by Adi Shankaracharya.

The Carnatic Wars and Its Impact on Kanchipuram

The Carnatic Wars (1746–1763) had a profound impact on the region, particularly Kanchipuram, which suffered from the extensive destruction caused by the British East India Company and the French East India Company. These wars were part of the global struggle for colonial dominance, and the subsequent instability forced religious institutions, including the Kanchi Kamakoti Mutt, to relocate temporarily to Kumbakonam.

The Three Carnatic Wars & Their Impact on Kanchipuram

- **First Carnatic War (1746–1748)**: This conflict saw the **French** capturing **Madras**, which was later returned to the British after the **Treaty of Aix-la-Chapelle**. Kanchipuram witnessed significant military activity during this period.
- **Second Carnatic War (1749–1754)**: The rivalry between **British-backed Muhammad Ali** and **French-backed Chanda Sahib** for control over **Arcot** escalated into full-blown conflict. The military movements made Kanchipuram unsafe for religious gatherings.
- **Third Carnatic War (1757–1763)**: As part of the **Seven Years' War**, the British, under **General Sir Eyre Coote**, defeated the French at **Vandavasi வந்தவாசி**, leading to the fall of French power. However, the proximity of Kanchipuram to **Arcot** and **Madras** kept it vulnerable, forcing religious institutions to relocate for safety.

The Kanchi Kamakoti Mutt's Relocation to Kumbakonam

With the violence of the wars escalating, the Kanchi Mutt made the bold decision to relocate to Kumbakonam. This was not merely a relocation but a spiritual safeguard for the future. The relocation ensured the preservation of the golden idol of Goddess Kamakshi, an object of immense spiritual importance, while ensuring the continuity of the Kanchi Kamakoti Peetam's sacred mission.

The Secrecy Behind the Journey

The relocation of the golden Kamakshi idol had to be carried out with utmost secrecy to prevent any potential threats from invaders or thieves. A small, trusted group of disciples and priests was selected to undertake the journey. The idol was carefully concealed inside a palanquin, disguised as a regular pilgrimage, and the group set out, traveling through hidden forest paths and village trails to avoid detection.

Their journey took them to Udayarpalayam, then to Thanjavur, and ultimately to Kumbakonam, where the Kanchi Kamakoti Peetam at Tanjavur. The golden Kamakshi idol was safely enshrined, and the Mutt resumed its mission of preserving the teachings of Advaita Vedanta and Sanatana Dharma in the spiritually rich environment of Kumbakonam.

Why Kumbakonam?

Kumbakonam was chosen not just for its safety but also for its profound spiritual significance. Known as the "Temple City", Kumbakonam had long been a center of learning, spirituality, and religious practice. The sacred waters of the Kaveri River and the revered temples of Kumbeshwarar and Mangalambal were considered to possess extraordinary spiritual powers, making it an ideal location for the Mutt's relocation. It was believed that a pilgrimage to Kumbakonam could absolve sins committed in other holy cities like Kashi.

The Sacred Sloka of Kumbakonam

The spiritual significance of Kumbakonam is underscored in the revered Sloka that highlights its purifying power:

"काशी कुम्भकोणं च गंगायमुनया युतं। तत्र स्नात्वा सदा पुण्यं धर्मं यः कर्तुमर्हति।"

"Kashi Kumbhakonam cha Gangayamunayā Yutam, Tatra Snātvā Sadā Puṇyaṃ Dharmaṃ Yaḥ Kartumarhati."

This Sloka emphasizes that the act of bathing in the Kaveri River and worshiping Kumbeshwarar and Mangalambal in Kumbakonam absolves the sins of those who have visited Kashi (Varanasi), bringing them spiritual purification.

The Sacred Connection Between Adi Shankaracharya and Kumbakonam

The roots of Adi Shankaracharya's legacy also run deep in the region of Kumbakonam. Shankaracharya, born in Kalady (Kerala), had strong ties to Sri Sivagurunatha Swamy Temple at Shivapuram near Kumbakonam, where his family hailed from. His spiritual lineage is inextricably linked with the Shiva Guru tradition, and the teachings of Advaita Vedanta continue to resonate in Kumbakonam and the surrounding regions.

Return to Kanchipuram

Though the Kanchi Kamakoti Mutt had relocated to Kumbakonam for nearly two centuries, its connection to Kanchipuram remained unbroken. In 1960, under the guidance of the 68th Peetadhipathi, Sri Chandrasekarendra Saraswathi Swamigal, the Mutt formally returned to Kanchipuram, restoring its spiritual heritage and solidifying its place as a beacon of wisdom and devotion for generations to come.

Through unwavering faith and divine grace, the golden Kamakshi idol was preserved at Tanjavur, ensuring that her blessings would continue to shine upon the world, illuminating the path of Sanatana Dharma.

ॐ

04

THE DIVINE CORONATION AND FIRST YATRA

The Sacred Pattabhishekam at Kumbakonam

As discussed in the previous chapter, on **May 7, 1907**, the coronation (*Pattabhishekam*) of the young Swaminathan as the **68ᵗʰ Peetadhipathi** of **Kanchi Kamakoti Peetam** took place at the sacred Kumbakonam Mutt. This grand event was attended by devotees, royal dignitaries—including the Maharaja of Tanjavur—government officials, and eminent scholars.

Many years later, after 75 years, Maha Periyava himself recounted the divine manner in which his coronation was conducted.

The ceremony began with elaborate Vedic rituals, as revered scholars and priests from across India assembled to invoke divine blessings. The young Swamiji was seated on a sacred Sinhasana, and the senior priests of the Mutt performed *Abhishekam* (holy anointment) with water brought from India's most sacred rivers—Ganga, Yamuna, Godavari, Kaveri, and Other Rivers. As the sacred waters cascaded over the young Acharya, the air vibrated with the powerful chants of the Sri Rudram, Chamakam, Purusha Suktam, etc., invoking the divine presence of the Almighty.

The sacred Peetam (throne), adorned with golden silk, was then sanctified, and Swamiji was ceremoniously seated upon it as Sri Chandrasekarendra Saraswati Swamigal—the new Jagadguru of the Kanchi Kamakoti Peetam.

Royal Patronage and the Divine Procession

Among the many dignitaries present, the Maharaja of Tanjavur played a crucial role. A staunch devotee of the Kanchi Mutt, the Maharaja arrived in regal splendor, accompanied by a grand royal procession of elephants, horses, and musicians. As a mark of utmost reverence, he offered a magnificently decorated elephant-drawn chariot to Maha Periyava for the Pattina Pravesam (ceremonial procession through the town).

This divine chariot, adorned with golden embellishments and intricate carvings of Hindu deities, was dedicated to the Acharya for spiritual processions. The gathered devotees were awestruck as the majestic elephants, draped in golden silk and studded with jewel-adorned headpieces, bowed in reverence before the Acharya, acknowledging his divine stature.

The Enchanting Music and Floral Offerings

The coronation was further elevated by the mesmerizing strains of Carnatic music that filled the sacred atmosphere. Renowned Nadaswaram and Thavil vidwans played auspicious *ragas* such as Gambhira Nattai, Mohanam, and Shankarabharanam, symbolizing spiritual victory and divine grace. The powerful beats of the Thavil reverberated through the temple corridors, while the royal brass band played a unique fusion of Carnatic and Western classical tunes, adding a majestic aura to the occasion.

As the *Pattabhishekam* reached its grand culmination, devotees, scholars, and royalty came forward to offer fragrant Jasmine flowers—a rare variety with an exquisite divine fragrance that lingers for days. The temple corridors overflowed with large baskets of jasmine, lotus, and roses, symbolizing devotion and reverence for the new Acharya.

Despite the grandeur of the coronation, Maha Periyava embodied humility. Even as a young Acharya, he displayed remarkable wisdom and detachment, ensuring that the royal donations were used solely for Vedic learning, temple services, and public welfare. His personal oversight led to the establishment of Veda Patashalas, charitable institutions, and spiritual outreach programs, thus keeping Sanatana Dharma vibrant and accessible to all.

A Journey Through Thindivanam – A Childhood Connection

As Maha Periyava traveled from Kalavai to Kumbakonam Mutt for his coronation, his journey took him through Thindivanam, his early residential town.

The people of Thindivanam, who had once seen Swaminathan as a child playing in the streets, were overjoyed to witness him return as the Acharya of Shankara Mutt. The entire village gathered at the entrance, offering a grand reception filled with devotion and reverence.

Among those awaiting him was an old woman known as Murukku Patti, who had once sold murukku (a crunchy, savory snack) to Swaminathan in his childhood. A light-hearted yet profound incident from his youth involved her. Young Swaminathan, who loved her murukkus, often brought his friends to buy from her. One day, he jokingly demanded a discount for bringing her so many customers.

Murukku Patti firmly declined, saying, *"The price is the same for everyone. Business must not be partial."*

Swaminathan playfully declared that he would never buy from her again, and she retorted, *"Do you think my business will suffer because of you? Do you expect me to receive you with a Poorna Kumbham (a sacred welcoming ritual) for you to visit my shop?"*

Years later, as he returned to Thindivanam as the Acharya, the entire village, including Murukku Patti, prepared to receive him with Poorna Kumbham. She hesitated, recalling their past conversation. Would he accept her offering?

As Periyava's palanquin reached her house, she was overwhelmed with emotions. As she humbly offered the Poorna Kumbham, Periyava accepted it with a smile, took the sacred coconut from the top, and placed it beside him in the palanquin. This moment symbolized divine forgiveness, wisdom, and the unwavering bond between the Guru and his devotees.

Sri Maha Periyava in Thiruvanaikaval, Trichy 1908

The First Yatra – A Pilgrimage to Thiruvanaikoil

Following the *Pattabhishekam*, Maha Periyava performed Vyasa Pooja at the Kumbakonam Mutt. Shortly thereafter, in February 1908, he embarked on his first Yatra to Thiruvanaikoil in Trichy, where he visited the sacred Jambukeswarar Temple, home to Goddess Akilandeswari.

At this time, the temple was undergoing Kumbabishekam, a once-in-12-years consecration ritual. Kanadukathan S. Rama Chettiar family had contributed significantly to the temple's renovation. As per tradition, all major rituals in the temple were performed under the guidance of the Kanchi Kamakoti Peetadhipathi, necessitating Maha Periyava's presence.

Adi Shankaracharya and Akilandeswari's Transformation

The connection between Kanchi Kamakoti Peetam and Thiruvanaikoil dates back 2,500 years to the time of Adi Shankaracharya. During his travels across Bharat, Adi Shankara visited the Jambukeswarar Temple and observed that Goddess Akilandeswari, in her Ugra Swaroopam (fierce form), was difficult for ordinary devotees to approach. To transform her into a Shanta Swaroopam (peaceful form), Adi Shankara installed the Sri Chakra and Shiva Chakra Thadangams (sacred earrings with yantras) on the deity's ears, calming her divine energy.

A significant highlight of the ceremony was that Sri Sacchidananda Shivabhinava Narasimha Bharathi Mahaswamigal, the revered Jagadguru of Sringeri Sharada Peetham (who headed the Peetham from 1879 to 1912), also graced the event. The participation of both great saints made this Kumbabishekam a momentous occasion in spiritual history.

The *Pattabhishekam* of Maha Periyava was not merely a coronation but the dawn of a spiritual era that transformed Hindu Dharma. His first Yatra to Thiruvanaikoil was the beginning of a lifelong journey—one that would illuminate the world with his wisdom, humility, and unwavering devotion to Sanatana Dharma.

Following the successful completion of the Kumbabishekam, Maha Periyava embarked on a Yatra to Elayathangudi, a sacred site in Chettinad. This town is home to the Shiva Temple of Kailasanathar and Paramakalyani, which has deep spiritual ties to the Kanchi Kamakoti Peetham.

Elayathangudi holds a special place in the Peetham's history, as the 65th Acharya, Sri Sudarshana Mahadevendra Saraswathi Swamigal, visited this place during his Yatra in 1890. On March 20th, he attained Siddhi (spiritual liberation) in Elayathangudi. As per Shastric injunctions, his Adhishtanam (final resting place) was consecrated there with a Shiva Lingam.

To pay homage to his Poorvacharya, Maha Periyava made a pilgrimage to Elayathangudi immediately after completing the Kumbabishekam at Thiruvanaikoil, reaffirming his deep reverence for the spiritual lineage of the Kanchi Kamakoti Peetham.

Sri Maha Periyava at Tanjore while yatra – 1908

05

THE SPIRITUAL FOUNDATION OF MAHA PERIYAVA

The Parameshti Guru and the Sacred Yatra

Maha Periyava's spiritual lineage is deeply rooted in the teachings of the 65th Acharya of Kanchi Kamakoti Peetham, Sri Sudarshana Mahadevendra Saraswathi Swamigal, also known as Elayathangudi Periyava. Maha Periyava revered his Parameshti Guru and frequently worshipped at his Adhishthanam (Samadhi shrine), drawing spiritual strength and inspiration.

During his early years as the 68th Acharya of the Kanchi Kamakoti Peetham, Maha Periyava embarked on a yatra across Chettinad at the invitation of the Pudukkottai Raja. As the Kanchi Mutt was the Raja Guru for the Pudukkottai Samasthanam, the Raja expressed his devotion by hosting Maha Periyava for 15 days, performing Padha Pooja (ritual worship of the Guru's feet), and offering various services.

The 1909 Mahamaham: A Divine Convergence

After his visit to Pudukkottai, Maha Periyava continued his journey to Kumbakonam, where he witnessed the grand Mahamaham festival in 1909. Often referred to as the *Kumbh Mela of the South*, this festival, held once every 12 years, is of immense spiritual significance. The 1909 Mahamaham was particularly notable as it was the first after Maha Periyava's ascension as the 68th Acharya.

Thousands of saints, scholars, and devotees gathered at the sacred Mahamaham Tank to take a holy dip and in the Kaveri River, believed to cleanse sins and bestow liberation.

The festival was attended by prominent Acharyas, including the revered Jagadgurus of the Kanchi Peetham. The Thanjavur Maharaja, along with other kings and noblemen, contributed generously, offering gold, precious gems, and silk garments to the deities. The royal patronage ensured the festival's grandeur, with extensive arrangements made for visiting pilgrims. The Kanchi Mutt conducted *Annadanam* (free food offerings) for thousands of devotees, reinforcing its role as a pillar of dharma and service.

The Acharya of Sarvagya Peetam

Maha Periyava, now the head of the *Sarvagya Peetam* (Throne of All-Knowing Wisdom), carried the responsibility of upholding the spiritual and Vedantic authority established by Adi Shankaracharya. The *Sarvagya Peetam* in Kanchipuram is revered as the ultimate seat of Advaita Vedanta, where Adi Shankara himself had once consolidated his teachings. As the Jagadguru, Maha Periyava was expected to master not only Vedic knowledge but also all worldly disciplines, embodying the wisdom required to guide seekers on their spiritual path.

Vidyabhyasam: The Rigorous Spiritual Education (1909–1914)

Maha Periyava commenced his formal education in 1909 at the Kumbakonam Mutt. His studies covered the *Vedas*, *Vedanta*, *Shastras*, and classical Sanskrit literature. His linguistic abilities extended beyond Sanskrit, as he also mastered English, French, Marathi, and Tamil. His Tamil literary studies included the sacred hymns of *Thevaram, Thiruvasagam, Thiruppugazh*, as well as epics like *Kamba Ramayanam* and *Periyapuranam*.

As the daily rituals of the Kanchi Mutt—such as the *Chandramouleeswara Pooja*—attracted numerous devotees, the senior scholars realized that Kumbakonam's bustling environment might not be conducive to uninterrupted learning. To ensure Maha Periyava's undisturbed education, they decided to move him to a secluded location.

Photo: During his Vidyabhyasam at Mahendramangalam 1910

The Solitude of Mahendramangalam

From 1911 to 1914, Maha Periyava was taken to Mahendramangalam, where he pursued intense spiritual studies in solitude. Here, he observed *Chatur Masya Vrata* (a four-month spiritual retreat) for three years and also embarked on his first *Padhayatra* (spiritual foot pilgrimage).

A devout follower, Sri Singam Iyengar of Srirangam, offered his bungalow as Maha Periyava's residence during this period. Remarkably, the bungalow remains preserved in its original form, serving as a testimony to this crucial phase of Maha Periyava's spiritual evolution.

Photo: Maha Periyava stayed in Sri Singam Iyengar's bungalow during Vidyabhyasam at Mahendramangalam 1910

The Illustrious Gurus of Maha Periyava

Maha Periyava's education was shaped by some of the most eminent scholars of his time. Among them, two were particularly significant:

Sri Sastraratnakara Mahamahopadhyaya Thiruvisanallur Sri Venkatasubba Sastrigal

Venkatasubba Sastrigal imparted not only Vedic knowledge but also the intricate teachings of *Vedanta, Brahma Sutras, Upanishads*, and *Sanskrit grammar*. His guidance was instrumental in shaping Maha Periyava's intellectual and spiritual depth. His method of teaching went beyond mere recitation; he emphasized deep contemplation and practical application of scriptural wisdom. Maha Periyava's humility and reverence for his guru remained steadfast throughout his life, often acknowledging the invaluable lessons he received.

Mahamahopadhyaya Painganadu Sri Ganapathy Sastrigal

A disciple of Mannargudi Periyava, Ganapathy Sastrigal was a renowned scholar in *Vedanta, Sanskrit, and Vedic rituals*. Under his mentorship, Maha Periyava mastered the intricate recitations and philosophical interpretations of the Vedas. His teachings extended beyond academic learning, focusing on spiritual discipline and unwavering commitment to *Sanatana Dharma*. The clarity with which Maha Periyava later guided devotees and scholars alike can be traced back to the wisdom imparted by his revered teachers.

The Divine Incident: Water Flowing Uphill

Even during his early years of learning, Maha Periyava's extraordinary wisdom was evident. In 1965, while observing *Chaturmasyam* in Kattupalli near Ennore, Maha Periyava recollected an incident from his Vidyabhyasam days at the age of 15.

One day, as Maha Periyava was preparing for his lesson in the Mutt's garden, Ganapathy Sastrigal approached him and performed *Namaskaram* (prostration). When Maha Periyava picked up his *Danda* (staff) to proceed with the day's lesson, the guru unexpectedly requested permission to leave. When asked why, Sastrigal cryptically replied, "Water will not flow from bottom to top."

Sensing that his guru was troubled, Maha Periyava remained silent, allowing him to express his concern. Sastrigal reiterated his statement, implying that a Guru could not teach a *Jagadguru*. He then explained, "Though I am teaching the Vedas and Upanishads, my student is the Guru of the Universe. A Guru cannot teach a *Sarvagya* (omniscient being)."

He revealed that on the first day of the lesson, he had observed Maha Periyava playing with river sand while listening, which he interpreted as inattentiveness. However, Maha Periyava, with his characteristic humility, assured his Guru that he had absorbed every word. To prove this, Maha Periyava invited his teacher to test him on the previous day's lessons. Upon answering every question with perfection, Ganapathy Sastrigal was overwhelmed with emotion and exclaimed, *"I have witnessed the impossible—water flowing uphill."* With tearful eyes, he sought Maha Periyava's permission to return to his village, convinced that no one was required to teach the *Sarvagya.*

Return to Kumbakonam: The Dawn of a Spiritual Leader

Upon completing his Vidyabhyasam, Maha Periyava returned to Kumbakonam, fully prepared to uphold the spiritual and administrative responsibilities of the Kanchi Kamakoti Mutt. His unparalleled wisdom, combined with his deep humility and devotion, marked the beginning of his extraordinary spiritual leadership.

This chapter of Maha Periyava's life stands as a testament to the significance of *Guru-Shishya Parampara* (teacher-student lineage) and the divine grace that shaped him into the guiding light of *Sanatana Dharma.*

Photo: Maha Periyava doing Japam in Kavery River Bank in 1911

Photo: During his Vidyabhyasam at Mahendramangalam 1912

Photo: *During his Vidyabhyasam at Mahendramangalam 1914*

Photo: During his Vidyabhyasam at Mahendramangalam 1914

ॐ

06

THE GRAND NAVARATRI UTSAVAM OF 1915

A Testament to Devotion and Service

In 1914, Maha Periyava completed his Vidyabhyasam (spiritual education) and returned to Kumbakonam. From 1911 to 1915, the management of the Kanchi Mutt was overseen by the District Court, which had appointed a guardian since Maha Periyava was still a minor. On 15th May 1915, upon attaining the age of 21, the complete administration of the Mutt was entrusted to him.

As per the traditions of Sannyasis, Mathathipathis (spiritual heads) do not directly engage in administrative tasks or sign documents. Instead, they appoint a Sri Karyam (Administrator) and an Agent who manage the Math's affairs with delegated authority. After assuming charge, Maha Periyava appointed Thirupathiripuliyur Pasupathi Iyer as Sri Karyam and Agent. Pasupathi Iyer, in an act of supreme devotion, refused any remuneration and dedicated his service to the Mutt as an offering of Seva.

Photo: Periyava taking charge in Kumbakonam Mutt in 1915

The First Grand Celebration – Shankara Jayanthi & The Birth of *Arya Dharmam*

The first major festival celebrated at the Mutt after Maha Periyava took charge was Shankara Jayanthi in 1915. This event was conducted on a grand scale, setting the precedent for future celebrations.

During this period, Maha Periyava initiated a monthly journal called *Arya Dharmam*, which was later widely circulated and reached thousands of readers. This publication, printed by Vani Vilas Press in Srirangam under the stewardship of T.K. Balasubramanya Iyer, played a significant role in propagating Sanatana Dharma.

The Grand Navaratri Utsavam of 1915

One of the most significant milestones of Maha Periyava's early years as the Acharya of the Kanchi Kamakoti Peetam was the Navaratri Utsavam of 1915 in Kumbakonam. This celebration was a testament to his deep devotion, meticulous planning, and the unwavering support of his devotees. The scale of the festivities was unprecedented, both in its spiritual significance and its community service.

Highlights of the 1915 Navaratri Utsavam

1. **Laksha Deepa Alankaram – 1 Lakh Lamps Illuminating Kumbakonam Mutt.**

   - Under Maha Periyava's guidance, one lakh lamps (*Laksha Deepam*) were lit across Kumbakonam Mutt, symbolizing the victory of Dharma over Adharma.
   - Devotees from across Tamil Nadu and South India participated, turning the town into a luminous beacon of spirituality.
   - The mesmerizing sight of these lamps enhanced the divine grandeur of the festival.

2. **Massive Annadhanam – Feeding 1 Lakh Devotees**

   - Maha Periyava organized *Annadhanam* (mass feeding) for over one lakh devotees throughout the festival.
   - The menu included *sambar*, rice, *payasam* (sweet pudding), and buttermilk, ensuring that every devotee was well-fed.

- o The event emphasized the Mutt's unwavering commitment to Dharma and service.

3. **Grand Chandramouleeswara Pooja & Special Navaratri Alankarams**

   - o Maha Periyava performed elaborate *Chandramouleeswara Pooja*, invoking the blessings of Lord Shiva.
   - o Each day witnessed special *Alankarams* (decorations) for Goddess Kamakshi and Chandramouleeswara, adorned with rare gems, silk, and gold ornaments.

4. **Royal & Devotee Contributions**

   - o Kings and Zamindars, including the Tanjore Maharaja, Pudukkottai Raja, and various South Indian Zamindars, generously contributed gold, silver, and funds.
   - o Wealthy families and common devotees alike donated wholeheartedly, making the event a community-driven divine effort.

5. **Vedic Chanting & Carnatic Music**

   - o Maha Periyava invited eminent Vedic scholars to chant *Devi Mahatmyam* (Durga Saptashati), *Rudram*, and *Upanishads*.
   - o Renowned Carnatic musicians performed daily, adding a divine ambiance to the celebrations.

6. **Maha Prasadam & Special Yagnas**

   - o Each of the nine days of Navaratri witnessed different offerings to Devi and Lord Chandramouleeswara.
   - o conducted sacred *Homams* (fire rituals), including:
     - ▪ *Chandi Homam* – To seek Devi's grace
     - ▪ *Maha Rudra Yagam* – For universal peace

The Impact of the 1915 Navaratri Utsavam

- This grand festival elevated the prominence of the Kanchi Kamakoti Peetam in South India.
- The unprecedented *Annadhanam* showcased Maha Periyava's compassion and selfless service.
- The *Laksha Deepam* tradition became an inspiration for future Navaratri celebrations.
- Maha Periyava's vision of an inclusive and community-driven celebration strengthened the spiritual and cultural fabric of the region.

Annadhana Sivan – The Unsung Hero Behind the Grand Annadhanam

One of the key figures in organizing the massive *Annadhanam* of 1915 was Annadhana Sivan, a devout follower of Maha Periyava known for his selfless service.

Who Was Annadhana Sivan?

- A great *bhakta* (devotee) of Maha Periyava, he believed *Annadhanam* (feeding the needy) was the highest form of *Seva* (service).
- His name became synonymous with large-scale food offerings at temples and religious gatherings.

How Did He Feed 1 Lakh People?

1. **Unwavering Faith in Maha Periyava**

   - Annadhana Sivan saw Maha Periyava as Lord Parameshwara himself and took upon himself the responsibility of feeding all devotees.
   - With absolute faith, he assured Periyava that no devotee would leave hungry.

2. **Massive Support from Devotees and Donors**

   - Merchants, landlords, and wealthy devotees contributed vast quantities of rice, *dal*, ghee, vegetables, and jaggery.
   - Even poor households contributed whatever they could—some offered a handful of rice, others donated firewood and vegetables.

3. **Efficient Kitchen Setup & Volunteer Support**

   - A massive kitchen was set up near the Mutt, with over 500 volunteers working tirelessly.
   - Large *vattis* (cauldrons) and firewood stoves were arranged to prepare vast quantities of food.

4. **Serving All Without Distinction**

   - Everyone, from Vedic scholars and priests to common devotees and the destitute, was served with devotion.
   - The feeding continued throughout the nine days of Navaratri.

5. **Miraculous Continuity of Food Supply**

   - Despite initial concerns over food shortages, Maha Periyava blessed the initiative, ensuring that the food never ran out.

Maha Periyava's Blessings to Annadhana Sivan

After the grand celebrations, Maha Periyava blessed Annadhana Sivan, recognizing his unparalleled service.

He is believed to have said:

"Annadhanam is the greatest Dharma. What you have done is nothing short of feeding Parameshwara Himself through His devotees."

The Legacy of the 1915 Annadhanam

- The 1915 Navaratri *Annadhanam* remains one of the most historic food offerings in Kumbakonam's history.
- The tradition of *Annadhanam* at the Kanchi Mutt continues to this day, inspired by the devotion of Annadhana Sivan and the divine grace of Maha Periyava.
- This event exemplified the transformative power of devotion, service, and unwavering faith.

In the later years, Maha Periyava embarked on a yatra to Chennai, where he stayed for a while during the Mahamagam Utsavam. During this period, Annadhana Sivan, who had come to Chennai to collect donations for the temple, was aware that Maha Periyava was in the city. Eager to receive the darshan of the Periyava, he visited him and observed that Periyava's feet were covered with red rashes caused by mosquito bites.

With utmost respect and concern, Annadhana Sivan politely told Periyava, "You may have no attachment to your body, but this divine body and soul belong to the devotees. The healthier you remain, the longer we will have the opportunity to remain in the presence of this divine soul. Please take care of yourself and protect yourself from mosquito bites and other insects." He then offered a mosquito net to Periyava, requesting him to sleep inside it for protection.

Out of his love and affection for the devotee, Periyava accepted the offer, and for some time, he used the mosquito net. When Annadhana Sivan passed away, Maha Periyava remarked, "He never learned the Vedas, nor did he chant mantras, but through the act of Annadhanam (feeding the poor), he attained Moksha." These words of Periyava clearly show that Annadhanam holds immense spiritual value, and it was one of the path for Moksha. The image of Jaganmatha Annapoorani holding the Anna Patram (the vessel for food) symbolizes the profound significance of Annadhanam.

An interesting incident followed during the Navaratri Utsavam. A devotee, who was none other than the great poet Mahakavi Subramanya Bharathiyar, wrote a letter to Maha Periyava. In his letter, he pointed out that during the Navaratri celebrations, people often pray for timely rainfall, which is crucial for survival. He had learned that the Kumbakonam Mutt was celebrating the Navaratri festival in a grand manner and suggested that this should be adopted worldwide. He further expressed his gratitude to Maha Periyava for the valuable teachings conveyed through the celebrations, acknowledging the wisdom that the Mutt had imparted.

On Vijayadashami, Periyava participated in the Pattinaprevasam in a grand Elephant Ambari, which was arranged by the Chettinadu Nagarathars. This procession, known as the Vijaya Yatra, saw lakhs of devotees walking miles together in celebration. With this grand procession, the Navaratri festival concluded, signifying both spiritual and material victories.

From 1914 to 1918, Maha Periyava resided in Kumbakonam, and during this period, numerous interesting events took place. Scholars and devotees from all over India visited Periyava to engage in debates and discussions. The solutions and answers Periyava provided to their doubts and questions often left everyone in awe, showcasing his unparalleled wisdom. Even music scholars visited to seek guidance, and their musical queries were answered with clarity and depth. This reflected the vastness of Maha Periyava's knowledge, affirming him as a true Sarvagyaan, possessing omniscient wisdom in every domain.

07

PROMOTING SPIRITUAL AND TRADITIONAL VALUES IN EDUCATION (1917)

Maha Periyava observed that the school and college curriculum lacked spiritual and traditional teachings of India, leading to a generation unaware of its rich heritage. To address this, he organized an all-India essay writing competition in English for children. The topic given was **"Ways to Save and Enrich Sanatana Dharma in the Evolving World."**

Many students participated, and the top three were shortlisted and felicitated at the Mutt. The first prize was won by **V. R. Ramachandra Dikshitar,** who later became a professor at Madras University. This initiative was one of the many steps Maha Periyava took to instill spiritual thoughts in the younger generation and uphold **Sanatana Dharma.**

Photo: Periyava in Tanjore Palace in 1917

Photo: Periyava with the Royal Family of Tanjore Raja in 1917

Encouragement of Avadhanam Traditions

The Mutt frequently hosted **Sathavadhani** and **Ashtavadhani** scholars, who showcased their extraordinary intellectual abilities before Maha Periyava and received his blessings.

Sathavadhani (शतावधानी)

- "Satha" means hundred, indicating a far greater level of skill than an Ashtavadhani.
- A Sathavadhani can simultaneously handle hundred different intellectual or artistic challenges while maintaining complete concentration.
- This rare ability is considered a mark of genius, and only a few individuals in history have been recognized as Sathavadhanis.

Ashtavadhani (अष्टावधानी)

- "Ashta" means **eight,** and "Avadhani" refers to **one who** possesses focused attention.
- An Ashtavadhani can focus on eight different intellectual tasks simultaneously, such as composing poetry, solving puzzles, answering logical questions, and demonstrating linguistic prowess.
- This practice is particularly prevalent in Sanskrit and Telugu literary traditions.

During one such gathering, Maha Periyava asked his mutt sevadharis to record the answers given by these scholars. However, before they could, Periyava himself answered all the questions—demonstrating his own mastery as a Sathavadhani and Ashtavadhani at the age of just 24!

Periyava and the Wisdom of Brahmacharya

Once, a man named Ramamoorthy, who ran a circus company and was deeply interested in Yogabhyasam (the dedicated practice of yoga), came for Periyava's darshan. He posed several intricate questions about Yogabhyasam, all of which Maha Periyava answered with clarity and depth.

Deeply moved, Ramamoorthy remarked, **"I have seen the power of Brahmacharya in Maha Periyava. With that power, anything can be achieved in this world."**

Invitation from the King of Darbhanga (1917)

Many eminent scholars, kings, and musicians visited Maha Periyava for his blessings. Once, the King of Darbhanga embarked on a spiritual tour of South India and stayed at the Kumbakonam Mutt for three days. He was deeply moved by Periyava's wisdom and requested him to visit North India and bless the people there.

Periyava graciously accepted the invitation, and this was one of the reasons he undertook the Kashi Yatra in 1919.

Periyava and the Promotion of Music

Many great musicians sought Periyava's blessings and guidance. Among them was Sri Umayalpuram Swaminatha Iyer, a disciple of Mahavaidyanatha Sivan, who was part of the lineage of Saint Tyagaraja.

Another great musician, Veena Vidwan Thiru Sabeshiyer, regularly visited the Mutt with his father Vaithyanatha Iyer and brother Krishnamoorthy to play the veena before Maha Periyava and Chandramouleeswarar.

Whenever Sabeshiyer performed, crowds naturally gathered—not just to listen to music, but because it was played before Maha Periyava, making it an intensely divine experience.

One day, as Sabeshiyer played beautifully, his father praised him, saying, "Sabash! Sabash!" Periyava called Vaithyanatha Iyer aside and asked, "Is it appropriate to praise your own son in a public gathering? Shouldn't he be praised by others instead?"

Vaithyanatha Iyer immediately understood his mistake and apologized. Periyava explained that according to Shastra, appreciation should follow certain principles:

1. **One can praise only two entities directly**—God and Guru.
2. **Relatives should not be praised directly** but should be spoken of highly to others, so appreciation reaches them indirectly.
3. **Workers should be appreciated only after they complete their tasks,** and even then, moderately, so that they do not take it for granted.
4. **Parents should never overpraise their own children,** as it hinders their growth. Children should develop so that others recognize and praise their achievements.

Reviving the Art of Harikatha

On one Shankara Jayanthi, Periyava called Thirupazhanam Punjapakesava Bhagavathar, a scholar and expert in Harikatha, and asked him to narrate Shankara Vijayam in Harikatha format. Bhagavathar humbly admitted that he was not well-versed in the subject.

Periyava, however, insisted, and Punjabakesava Bhagavathar took up the challenge. He diligently studied Shankara Vijayam, prepared, and performed the narration in Mutt for five days.

Periyava was immensely pleased and lavishly rewarded him. This initiative not only enriched Harikatha as an art form but also demonstrated how Periyava encouraged and preserved traditional arts.

Maha Periyava's Mastery Over Modern Science

Maha Periyava's wisdom was not limited to spiritual and Vedic knowledge. Two renowned professors—Rajagopala Iyer (Physics) and Manika Nayakar (Mathematics)—frequently visited the Mutt to discuss various topics with Periyava.

One day, during a discussion, Periyava elaborated on Vaana Sastra (Aeronautics and Space Science). The professors were stunned at his deep understanding of a subject they had spent years studying in universities.

Curious, they asked, "How does Periyava know all this, despite renouncing the world at the age of 13?"

Periyava simply replied, "All this knowledge is already mentioned in our Shastras."

This display of vast intellect and wisdom is known as Medha Vilasam.

08

THE SIGNIFICANCE OF KASHI YATRA

Significance of Kashi Yatra and Ganga Mata

Periyava then set out on his Kashi Yatra. According to Hindu tradition, every Hindu should visit Kashi at least once in their lifetime.

Significance of Kashi Yatra – Why Every Hindu Should Undertake It

Kashi Yatra, or the pilgrimage to Varanasi (Kashi), holds immense spiritual, religious, and cultural significance in Hinduism. Kashi is considered the oldest and holiest city in the world, often referred to as *Moksha Puri*—the city of liberation. Every devout Hindu is encouraged to visit Kashi at least once in their lifetime to experience its divine energy and seek blessings for spiritual upliftment and salvation (Moksha).

1. Kashi – The City of Lord Shiva

Kashi is believed to be the eternal abode of Lord Shiva, where he grants liberation to devotees. According to Hindu scriptures, Kashi exists beyond time and remains untouched even during cosmic dissolution (*Pralaya*). The great saint Adi Shankaracharya glorified Kashi in his hymns, stating that one who takes refuge in Kashi under the grace of Lord Vishwanatha (Shiva) is freed from the cycle of birth and death.

2. The Power of Ganga Snanam (Holy Dip in River Ganga)

The Ganga River flowing through Kashi is revered as *Moksha Dayini* (the giver of liberation). It is believed that taking a holy dip in the Ganga at Kashi washes away all sins (*Papahara Snanam*). The Kashi Khand of Skanda Purana states that one who bathes in the Ganga and worships Kashi Vishwanath attains Sadgati (liberation and divine status). The mantra *"Har Har Gange"* is chanted by devotees as they immerse themselves in the sacred waters.

3. Kashi Vishwanath Darshan and Rudrabhishekam

The Kashi Vishwanath Jyotirlinga is one of the twelve sacred Jyotirlingas of Lord Shiva. A special ritual called Rudrabhishekam (offering sacred items like milk, honey, and bilva leaves to Shiva) is performed, and it is believed that anyone who worships Kashi Vishwanath with devotion will have their sins absolved and will attain Moksha. Many great saints, including Ramakrishna Paramahamsa, Swami Vivekananda, and Adi Shankaracharya, have visited and meditated in Kashi.

4. Performing Shraddha and Pind Daan at Manikarnika Ghat

Manikarnika Ghat, the cremation ground in Kashi, is considered the most auspicious place for the last rites of a person. It is believed that those who breathe their last in Kashi and receive Shiva's Taraka Mantra (liberation mantra) are granted direct Moksha. Performing Pind Daan (ritual offerings to ancestors) in Kashi ensures peace and salvation for departed souls. According to Garuda Purana, ancestors (Pitru Devatas) receive eternal liberation when their descendants perform rituals at Kashi.

5. Kashi, Gaya, and Prayag – The Ultimate Pilgrimage Circuit

The Triveni Sangam at Prayagraj (confluence of Ganga, Yamuna, and the invisible Saraswati), the Pind Daan at Gaya for ancestral liberation, and the Kashi Vishwanath Darshan together form the most sacred pilgrimage circuit in Hinduism. A Hindu who undertakes this journey is said to have fulfilled one of the highest duties in life, ensuring spiritual elevation for themselves and their ancestors.

6. The Spiritual and Mystical Energy of Kashi

Kashi is also the land of great sages and saints like Tulsidas, Kabir, Adi Shankaracharya, and Trailanga Swami. It is believed that the vibrations of the city resonate with Vedic chants and divine energy, making it an ideal place for meditation and self-realization. The spiritual atmosphere of Kashi inspires devotion and helps in attaining inner peace.

Conclusion – Why Every Hindu Should Go for Kashi Yatra

Kashi Yatra is not just a pilgrimage but a sacred journey towards self-purification, divine connection, and Moksha. Every Hindu should visit Kashi to seek the blessings of Lord Shiva, take a dip in the holy Ganga, perform Shraddha for ancestors, and experience the divine energy of the eternal city. Scriptures declare that "Kashi is not just a place; it is an experience of ultimate truth and liberation." Hence, a visit to Kashi is considered the fulfillment of one's spiritual duty (Dharma) and an important step towards eternal peace and salvation (Moksha).

Periyava Explained Spiritual Importance of Ganga Mata

Ganga Mata, the sacred river Ganga, is not just a physical river but a divine entity in Hinduism, revered as a goddess and purifier of all sins (*Papaharini*). She is considered the Mother of all existence, bestowing spiritual liberation (*Moksha*) and divine blessings upon those who worship her or take a dip in her holy waters.

1. Ganga Mata as the Divine Purifier

The Ganga is believed to carry divine nectar (*Amrita*) from the heavens, making her waters sacred and spiritually purifying. According to Hindu scriptures, even the worst of sins are washed away by a single dip in the holy river. The Bhagavata Purana states:

> *"Ganga snanam karishyami yathachittam shuddhaya me"*
> (*I bathe in the Ganga to purify my heart and soul.*)

This belief is why millions of devotees visit the Ganges to take a holy dip, especially during auspicious occasions like Makar Sankranti, Kumbh Mela, and Ganga Dussehra.

2. The Descent of Ganga – A Divine Blessing

The story of Ganga's descent (*Ganga Avataran*) is one of the most sacred legends in Hinduism. Ganga Mata was originally flowing in the celestial realm, and King Bhagiratha performed severe penance to bring her down to Earth to purify the souls of his ancestors. Lord Shiva, recognizing the force of her descent, caught her in his matted locks and gently released her onto Earth. This divine act not only blessed Earth with sacred water but also established Ganga as the eternal river of Dharma and Moksha.

3. Ganga – The River of Liberation (Moksha Dayini)

The Garuda Purana mentions that one who dies on the banks of the Ganga attains Moksha (liberation) without fail. This is why Kashi, Haridwar, and Prayagraj are among the most sacred places for Hindus, where they perform Antyeshti (final rites) and Pind Daan (ancestral offerings) for departed souls. The Manikarnika Ghat in Varanasi is considered the holiest cremation ground, where Lord Shiva himself whispers the Taraka Mantra (liberation mantra) into the ears of the departed, granting them Moksha.

4. Ganga Mata and the Power of Mantras

The mere chanting of Ganga Mata's names is said to cleanse the soul and invoke divine blessings:

- *Ganga Mata Ki Jai!* (Victory to Mother Ganga)
- *Om Shri Gange Namah!* (Salutations to the holy Ganga)

Saints and sages have meditated on her banks, reciting the Ganga Stotram:

"Jahnavi, Tripathaga, Bhagirathi cha Vishnupadi, Sita, Alakananda te namostu te!"
(O Holy Ganga, you are Jahnavi, the one who flows in three worlds, Bhagirathi, born from Vishnu's feet, and Alakananda – I bow to you!)

5. Ganga and the Path of Bhakti and Sadhana

Many saints and Yogis, including Adi Shankaracharya, Tulsidas, and Swami Vivekananda, have performed Tapasya (penance) on the banks of Ganga. It is believed that her waters carry the vibrations of thousands of years of Vedic chants and Sadhana, making it a place of deep spiritual energy.

6. The Symbol of Compassion and Divine Motherhood

Ganga Mata is worshipped as the divine mother, who embraces and accepts all beings without discrimination. Just as a mother forgives her children's mistakes, Ganga Mata cleanses devotees of their karmic burdens. This quality makes her one of the most compassionate and loving deities in Hinduism.

7. Conclusion – Why Every Devotee Must Worship Ganga Mata

The spiritual importance of Ganga Mata is beyond mere ritualistic worship. She represents purity, devotion, forgiveness, and liberation.

Every Hindu aspires to have a sacred bath in the Ganges, offer Arghya (water oblation) to the Sun God, and perform Ganga Aarti as an act of gratitude. Ganga is not just a river; she is the divine flow of spirituality, wisdom, and ultimate salvation.

Thus, it is said:

> *"Gange Tav Darshanat Mukti, Sparshanat Papanashanam, Snanat Swargamavapnoti, Stavanat Jnanam Apnuyat"*

(*By seeing you, one attains liberation; by touching you, sins are destroyed; by bathing in you, one reaches heaven; by praising you, one attains divine wisdom.*)

In the next section, we will explore Maha Periyava's **Kashi Yatra in depth.**

Photo: Periyava with Patasai Vidyartis in Kumbakonam in 1918

Maha Periyava often emphasized that every human being should undertake the Kashi Yatra at least once in their lifetime. His own Kashi Yatra spanned an extraordinary 21 continuous years, from 1919 to 1939, making it a unique and unparalleled spiritual journey in history. During this yatra, Maha Periyava:

- Visited and worshipped at numerous sacred temples across India.
- Took ritualistic baths in the holy rivers (Theertham).
- Visited thousands of villages and towns, giving darshan to millions of devotees.

His yatra was meticulously aligned with the Sastric (scriptural) guidelines of Kashi Yatra, as he demonstrated an unwavering commitment to Dharma, urging society to adhere to the Sastras.

As per Sastra, How one should do Kashi Yatra?

Before embarking on a Kashi Yatra, it is essential to follow prescribed rituals:

1. **Sankalpam & Anugnai:** A couple intending to undertake Kashi Yatra must first take a Sankalpam (spiritual resolution) and perform Vigneshwara Pooja. They must seek permission (Anugnai) from learned Vedic scholars (Veda Vidwans or Ved Vyasa) to neutralize ego and seek divine approval for their pilgrimage.

The Sacred Journey Begins: Rameshwaram & Devipatnam

1. **Uppur** (Near Rameshwaram): Lord Rama and Lakshmana installed and worshipped Maha Ganapathi here before their journey to Lanka, signifying the importance of invoking Ganesha's blessings before any auspicious journey.

2. **Devipatnam:** Worship of the **Navagrahas**, where Lord Rama installed **Navapashana** (nine planetary deities) to seek their blessings for his journey.

3. **Rameshwaram:** One of the 12 Jyotirlingas, where devotees take a holy dip at Dhanushkodi, collect a handful of sand, and later perform Pitru Tarpanam (ancestral rites). This ritual is believed to grant ancestral blessings and spiritual merit. Taking bath at the wells in Ramanathaswamy Temple, Dharshan of Sethumathavar.

Spiritual Significance of Pitru Tarpanam: Performing Pitru Tarpanam is not just a ritual but a profound spiritual duty that:

- Connects the past, present, and future generations.
- Ensures the upliftment of ancestors.
- Grants divine grace, abundance, peace, and spiritual progress across generations.

The Confluence of the Three Rivers: Prayagraj (Allahabad)

After Rameshwaram, the journey continues to Prayagraj (formerly Allahabad), where the holy confluence (Triveni Sangam) of Ganga, Yamuna, and the mystical Saraswati takes place.

Significance of Triveni Sangam:

- Mentioned in the Rigveda and Puranas as the King of Pilgrimage Sites (Teertharaja).
- Lord Brahma is believed to have performed the first Yagna here.
- The sacred Kumbh Mela is held here every 12 years.
- Bathing here is said to wash away sins and grant Moksha (spiritual liberation).
- Dharshan of Veni Madhavar, Root of Akshyavatam

Important Rituals at Prayagraj:

- **Veni Dhanam:** A ritual performed by husband & wife at Triveni Sangam, offering strands of their hair in prayer for their husband's long life.
- **Immersion of the Sand from Dhanushkodi:** The handful of sand collected from Dhanushkodi is immersed here, symbolizing the completion of a crucial step in the yatra.
- Phithru Sradham, Pindadhanam etc.

The Holy City of Kashi (Varanasi)

Upon reaching **Kashi**, devotees perform:

1. **Panch Ghata Snanam** (Sacred Bath in Five Ghats):

   - Symbolizes purification through the five elements (Pancha Bhootas).
   - Ritual offerings are made for ancestral liberation (Pithru Moksha).

2. **Darshan of Sacred Temples in Kashi:**

   - **Kashi Vishwanath Temple** – The presiding deity of Kashi.
   - **Annapurna Devi Temple** – Goddess of nourishment and prosperity.
   - **Kala Bhairav Temple** – Guardian deity of Kashi.
   - **Sankat Mochan Hanuman Temple** – Worshipped for removing obstacles.
   - **Durga Kund Temple** – Dedicated to Goddess Durga.
   - **Vishalakshi Temple** – One of the 51 Shakti Peethas.
   - **Mrityunjay Mahadev Temple** – Believed to grant protection from untimely death.
   - **Bindhu Madhavar Temple** – One of the 108 Divya Desams

The Sacred Rituals at Gaya

After Kashi, devotees travel to Gaya, where they worship Vishnupad Temple, which enshrines the footprint of Lord Vishnu.

Significance of Gaya and Vishnupad Temple:

- Gayasura's penance made the region so sacred that even sinners could attain Moksha.
- Lord Vishnu pressed his divine foot on Gayasura to restore cosmic balance, leaving behind his sacred footprint.
- The site is now one of the most important places for performing Pind Daan (ancestral offerings).

Other Sacred Sites in Gaya:

- **Akshaya Vatam (The Eternal Banyan Tree):**
  - Associated with Lord Vishnu and Brahma's Yagna.
  - Performing Pitru Tarpanam here grants eternal merit (Akshaya Punya).
  - Lord Rama and Goddess Sita performed Pind Daan for King Dasharatha at this site.

The Final Return to Rameshwaram

After completing Kashi Yatra, devotees return to Prayagraj and perform a final pooja as a couple, collecting sacred Ganga water to carry back to Rameshwaram.

Why Must One Visit Rameshwaram After Kashi Yatra?

1. **Completion of Ancestral Rites:** Kashi Yatra is considered **incomplete** without offering Ganga water at **Ramanathaswamy Temple**.

2. **Spiritual Significance:** The journey represents the **union of Shaivism (Kashi Vishwanath) and Vaishnavism (Rameshwaram, associated with Lord Rama)**.
3. **Final Purification:** Devotees take a **holy dip in the 22 Theerthams** at Rameshwaram to remove any remaining karma.

The final step involves performing Abhishekam to Lord Ramanathaswamy with the Ganga water brought from Prayagraj, followed by Ganga Pooja and Samaradhana at home, marking the successful completion of the sacred Kashi Yatra.

The Ultimate Path to Liberation

The Kashi Yatra is not just a physical journey but a spiritual odyssey that purifies the soul, liberates ancestors, and bestows divine blessings. By adhering to the Sastric guidelines and performing the prescribed rituals, one achieves:

- **Pithru Moksha** (ancestral salvation).
- **Purification of sins.**
- **Attainment of Moksha** (spiritual liberation).
- **Divine blessings for generations.**

May Maha Periyava's teachings continue to inspire generations to embark on this **sacred journey of self-purification and enlightenment**.

Photo: Periyava with Devotees in Kumbakonam in 1918

Photo: Periyava in 1918

Maha Periyava's Kashi Yatra was not just a pilgrimage but a momentous spiritual event deeply rooted in the sacred traditions of Sanatana Dharma. While ordinary mortals undertake the Kashi Yatra to cleanse themselves of sins by bathing in the holy waters of Ganga Mata, great Mahans, Sadhus, and Jagadgurus embark on this divine journey to sanctify Ganga Mata herself.

The Divine Purpose of Kashi Yatra

As per the ancient scriptures, the holy river Ganga descended to the earth from the heavens to purify the souls of mankind. Devotees immerse themselves in her waters to wash away their sins, leaving behind an accumulated burden of impurities. Realizing this, Ganga Mata, in deep anguish, sought Lord Shiva's guidance, asking how she could free herself from the burden of the sins she had absorbed.

Lord Shiva, in his infinite compassion, reassured her:

> *"Whenever your divine waters become overburdened with the sins of humanity, I shall manifest on this earth in the form of great Rishis, Sadhus, and Jagadgurus. These enlightened beings will cleanse you by taking a dip in your waters and thus restore your sanctity."*

Thus, the Kashi Yatra of Mahans is not for their own purification but to fulfill the divine command of Lord Shiva by purging Ganga Mata of the accumulated sins of countless devotees.

Maha Periyava's Kashi Yatra – A Journey of Cosmic Significance

In alignment with this sacred tradition, Maha Periyava undertook the Kashi Yatra with the highest spiritual intent. His journey was not one of necessity but of divine duty, ensuring the continued sanctity of the holiest river.

During his pilgrimage, Maha Periyava did not merely visit the sacred sites but also engaged in deep penance, performed Vedic rituals, and spread spiritual wisdom to those who sought his guidance. His presence itself was an act of purification, reaffirming the deep connection between Ganga Mata, Sanatana Dharma, and the great lineage of Jagadgurus.

Maha Periyava's arrival at Kashi was received with immense reverence. His deep knowledge of the Vedas, Upanishads, and Shastras was recognized by the scholars of Kashi, and his discourses on Advaita Vedanta further strengthened the spiritual fabric of the sacred city.

One of the most significant moments of his Yatra was his holy dip in the Ganga. The presence of such a great Tapasvi, a true embodiment of Dharma, restored the river's purity and reinforced her divine purpose.

The Eternal Message of the Kashi Yatra

Maha Periyava's Kashi Yatra serves as a beacon of wisdom for all seekers of truth. It teaches that true pilgrimage is not merely about visiting sacred places but about uplifting and contributing to the spiritual welfare of the universe. It is a reminder that Sanatana Dharma is deeply interconnected with nature, divinity, and selfless duty.

The profound impact of Maha Periyava's journey remains eternal, inspiring generations to undertake spiritual sadhana and uphold the sacred traditions of Bharata Varsha. Through his life and actions, he demonstrated that the greatest service to Dharma is not just in personal liberation but in uplifting the entire cosmos with divine grace and wisdom.

Thus, the sacred Kashi Yatra of Maha Periyava was not just an event but a cosmic act of sanctification—an offering to Ganga Mata, a fulfillment of Lord Shiva's promise, and a divine moment in the history of Sanatana Dharma.

$$\text{ॐ}$$

09

ANANTHAKRISHNA SHARMA: THE PATHFINDER OF PERIYAVA'S KASHI YATRA

The Miraculous Kashi Yatra: A Divine Journey of 21 Years

In the sacred history of Kanchi Maha Periyava, his legendary 21-year-long Kashi Yatra stands as an unparalleled spiritual journey in Hindu Dharma. Our Bharata Punya Bhoomi is adorned with countless holy temples and divine theerthams (sacred rivers and water bodies). To reveal the profound significance of these sacred sites, Periyava undertook this grand pilgrimage, traversing the length and breadth of the country in devotion.

Yet, behind this historic Yatra was an unsung hero—a devoted soul chosen by Periyava himself to prepare the path for this divine mission. His name was Tenkasi Ananthakrishna Sharma.

The Preparation for Kashi Yatra: A Divine Test

Though Periyava formally embarked on his Kashi Yatra in 1919, the meticulous planning began nearly seven years earlier. Recognizing the immense challenges of such an extensive pilgrimage, Periyava sought a pathfinder—someone who could journey ahead, chart the routes, identify key places, and ensure a smooth passage.

Thus, in an extraordinary decision, Periyava sent Ananthakrishna Sharma to Kashi on a pilot Yatra, entrusting him with the sacred responsibility of paving the way. However, this was no ordinary assignment. The selection process for this role was both rigorous and spiritually demanding, defined by a set of strict conditions that tested one's faith, endurance, and detachment from worldly comforts.

The Ten Sacred Conditions for the Pilot Yatra

One day, Periyava gathered his devotees and expressed his wish to send a sevak (disciple) on this preparatory Yatra. Many were eager for the divine opportunity, but when they heard the conditions, they realized it was an almost impossible task. The ten conditions laid down by Periyava were as follows:

1. The journey must be undertaken entirely on foot—from Kumbakonam to Kashi.
2. The traveler must go alone; no companions were allowed. Additionally, he had to cook his own food throughout the journey.
3. Only raw materials obtained through Bhiksha (alms) were permitted—cooked food was not to be accepted from anyone. Periyava believed that cooking one's own food fosters simplicity and self-discipline.
4. Consumption of coffee and tea was strictly prohibited, as Periyava regarded them as addictive habits.
5. The traveler must carry minimal belongings, ensuring ease of movement and a spirit of renunciation.
6. No money was to be accepted or asked for at any point during the journey.
7. Continuous movement was essential—he could only stay at one place for a single night, unless illness prevented travel.
8. Though he could inform people that he was on this Yatra under Periyava's instructions, he could not carry any proof or letter from the Mutt to seek favors or privileges.

9. He must carry ample postcards and a pencil, regularly sending detailed updates about his journey and the places he visited to the Mutt.

10. By the time he reached Kashi, he must have learned Hindi, ensuring he could communicate effectively in the holy city.

The return journey, however, could be completed by train.

A Young Devotee Accepts the Divine Challenge

Upon hearing these stringent conditions, most devotees hesitated, realizing the difficulty of such a journey. But one young man—just 20 years old—stepped forward with unwavering faith and devotion. It was Tenkasi Ananthakrishna Sharma, a steadfast devotee of Maha Periyava. Without hesitation, he accepted all the conditions and prepared himself for the arduous journey ahead.

With Periyava's blessings, Sharma embarked on this incredible Yatra, walking thousands of kilometers over a period of six months. True to his word, he meticulously followed every instruction, sending detailed postcards documenting his experiences. Upon reaching Kashi, he completed his mission and returned by train, successfully fulfilling Periyava's divine command.

Periyava's 21-Year Kashi Yatra Begins

Every step of this journey was marked by divine grace and profound spiritual experiences.

The postcards sent by Ananthakrishna Sharma, serving as sacred records of this remarkable journey.

A Test of Faith: The Vindhya Mountains Incident

During his journey, Sharma encountered many hardships and miraculous experiences. One such incident took place in the Vindhya mountain range (Vindhyachal) of Madhya Pradesh. While passing through a dense forest with no shelter in sight, he came across large water pipes stacked by the roadside. With no other option, he crawled inside one of the pipes to rest for the night.

As darkness fell, the jungle echoed with the roars of tigers and lions prowling nearby. Fear gripped him, but he surrendered himself to Periyava's divine protection. Praying fervently, he remained unharmed and safely resumed his journey at dawn.

A Legacy of Devotion and Sacrifice

The successful completion of this pilot Yatra laid the foundation for Periyava's own divine mission. For 21 long years, Periyava traveled across the sacred land of Bharat, sanctifying countless places with his presence and reviving the essence of Sanatana Dharma.

Tenkasi Ananthakrishna Sharma's selfless dedication and unwavering devotion made him an integral part of this historic journey. His sacrifice and discipline stand as a testament to the power of faith and obedience to one's Guru.

Through this unparalleled Yatra, Periyava not only revealed the spiritual significance of our holy land but also exemplified the virtues of discipline, detachment, and devotion—leaving behind a legacy that continues to inspire generations.

10

THE SIGNIFICANCE OF CHATURMASYA AND PERIYAVA'S KASI YATRA 1919

The Sannyasi's Eternal Journey: The Need for Constant Yatra

According to the Shastras, a Sannyasi (renunciate) is beyond the bonds of relationships and worldly attachments. To maintain this detachment, a Sannyasi is required to constantly travel (yatra), ensuring they do not become attached to any place, people, or atmosphere.

However, during the period of Chaturmasya (four sacred months), they must stay in one place and perform spiritual practices and rituals. The primary reasons for this are:

1. **Practical Reasons – The Monsoon Season**

    o   In India, the months from Aani to Karthikai (June to November) mark the rainy season.

    o   To avoid the difficulties of traveling during heavy rains, Sannyasis observe Chaturmasya Vratham by staying in a single location.

2. **Compassion and Non-Violence (Ahimsa)**

    o   The monsoon season gives life to countless insects and tiny creatures that appear on the ground.

- ○ Traveling during this time could harm these beings, violating the principle of Ahimsa (non-violence)—a fundamental tenet of Sannyasa Dharma.

The Core Principles of Sannyasa Dharma

The life of a Sannyasi is guided by three fundamental principles:

- **Ahimsa (Non-Violence):** Ensuring no harm is caused by thoughts, words, or actions.
- **Brahmacharya (Celibacy and Self-Restraint):** Maintaining purity in body and mind to attain spiritual enlightenment.
- **Aparigraha (Non-Possession):** Detachment from material wealth, living with minimal needs, and depending on divine providence.

The Spiritual Essence of Chaturmasya Vratham

Observing Chaturmasya Vratham is not just about renouncing travel but also about deepening spiritual discipline, intensifying self-restraint, and focusing on inner purification.

Maha Periyava's adherence to Chaturmasya Vratham was marked by strict austerities and progressive renunciation of different food items every month.

First Month – Sāga Vratham (Strict Diet Without Vegetables and Fruits)

- **Abstained from:** All vegetables and fruits.
- Purpose: To symbolize detachment from taste and luxury, emphasizing simple and minimalistic living.

Second Month – Dadhi Tyaga (Avoidance of Curd and Buttermilk)

- **Abstained from:** Curd and buttermilk, considered rich and nourishing foods.

- **Purpose:** Self-restraint and inner purification by renouncing indulgence in comfort foods.

Third Month – Ksheera Tyaga (Abstinence from Milk and Dairy Products)

- **Abstained from:** Milk and all dairy products.
- **Purpose:** To practice deeper self-discipline and reduce bodily dependency on external nourishment, relying more on spiritual energy.

Fourth Month – Dvithalam Virutham (Avoidance of Pulses and Seeds)

- **Abstained from:** All lentils (Paruppu), pulses, and seeds, which are major protein sources.
- **Purpose:** To enter the most rigorous stage of detachment from worldly sustenance, allowing the body and mind to focus solely on divine consciousness.

Maha Periyava's 1919 Chaturmasya Vratham at Veppathur, Tamil Nadu

Maha Periyava first undertook 1919 Chaturmasya Vratham in Vepathur, Tamil Nadu. This tradition began on Ashada Pournami (Guru Purnima) and continued until Karthikai month in the Tamil calendar.

Vyasa Pooja on Ashada Pournami – Honoring the Guru Parampara

The Spiritual Significance of Ashada Pournami (Guru Purnima)

Ashada Pournami, or Guru Purnima, is an auspicious day dedicated to honoring the Guru Parampara—the lineage of spiritual masters who have preserved and imparted Vedic wisdom.

- This day marks the birth anniversary of Bhagavan Veda Vyasa, the sage who classified the Vedas, authored the Mahabharata, and composed the Puranas.

- Vyasa Pooja is performed to express gratitude to the Guru lineage and reaffirm devotion to the Guru-Sishya (Master-Disciple) tradition.

Maha Periyava's Observance of Vyasa Pooja

Maha Periyava performed Vyasa Pooja with meticulous discipline, following traditional rituals that included:

1. **Guru Vandana (Honoring the Guru Lineage)**

   - Invoked the blessings of Veda Vyasa, Adi Shankaracharya, and the Advaita Acharyas.
   - Offered sacred prayers and chanted Vedic hymns to honor them.

2. **Vedantic Discourses and Teachings**

   - Delivered spiritual discourses on the importance of Guru Bhakti (devotion to the Guru) and Advaita Vedanta.

3. **Annadanam (Offering of Food)**

   - Maha Periyava arranged large-scale food distribution (Annadanam) for ascetics, brahmacharis, and the needy.
   - He emphasized that serving food to the hungry is the highest form of Guru Seva (service to the Guru).

4. **Acceptance of Bhiksha (Sacred Alms)**

   - As per Sannyasa Dharma, Maha Periyava **accepted Bhiksha (alms) from devotees**, reinforcing the principle of **renunciation and detachment**.

The Spiritual Essence of Vyasa Pooja

The Eternal Role of the Guru

- The **Guru** is the dispeller of **darkness (Avidya)** and the illuminator of **true knowledge (Jnana)**.
- The chanting of **Guru Stotram** and offering of prayers **strengthen the bond between Guru and disciple**.

Guru's Grace as the Ultimate Blessing

- Seeking the blessings of the **Guru on Ashada Pournami** bestows **immense spiritual merit** and helps seekers overcome obstacles.

Maha Periyava's Message on Guru Purnima

Maha Periyava often emphasized:

"A true disciple must cultivate humility, unwavering faith, and gratitude for the Guru. The Guru's teachings should not remain in books but be lived in daily life."

Through his strict adherence to tradition, deep wisdom, and devotion, Maha Periyava preserved the sanctity of Vyasa Pooja, reinforcing the timeless Guru-Sishya Parampara.

After completing Chaturmasya Vratham in Vepathur, Maha Periyava visited Thiruvarur in 1920, a sacred Shaiva Kshetram known for its Mooladhara Chakra energy.

(Next, we will explore Maha Periyava's visit to Thiruvarur and the significance of Tyagaraja Swamy.)

Maha Periyava's Visit to Thiruvarur

After completing the Chaturmasya Vratham in Vepathur in 1919, Maha Periyava continued his divine yatra, reaching the sacred town of Thiruvarur in 1920. Thiruvarur, one of the holiest Shaiva Kshetrams, holds immense spiritual, historical, and cultural significance. It is revered as the Adi Peetam of Shiva worship and is deeply associated with Shaiva Siddhanta.

Thiruvarur – The Mooladhara Kshetram

Thiruvarur is known as the Mooladhara Kshetram, representing the Mooladhara Chakra, the foundational energy center in the human body. This sacred site is believed to be a powerful place for spiritual awakening and Kundalini Shakti activation. A grand shrine dedicated to Lord Shiva in his Somaskanda form, where the Lord is worshipped as Sri Tyagaraja Swamy. Birth place of Sangeetha Thirumoorthis Sri Thagarajar, Sri Muthuswamy Diskitar and Sri Shyama Sastrigal.

The Grand Reception for Maha Periyava

As Maha Periyava entered Thiruvarur, the town's people gathered in large numbers to welcome him with great reverence and devotion. The entire region was filled with divine fervor, and Vedantic chants, bhajans, and traditional music echoed through the air. Thousands of devotees had arrived from different parts of Tamil Nadu, eager to have Periyava's darshan and blessings.

Wherever Maha Periyava traveled, a retinue of over 200 dedicated followers would walk alongside his palanquin (pallakku). These followers included Vedic scholars, disciples, caretakers, and administrators, who ensured the smooth flow of the yatra. Along with them, a vast entourage of cows, elephants, and horses accompanied Periyava, symbolizing the grand spiritual procession of the Kanchi Kamakoti Peetam.

Sri Tyagaraja Swamy Temple – The Heart of Thiruvarur

At the heart of Thiruvarur lies the Sri Tyagaraja Swamy Temple, a divine center of Shaiva worship. This temple is unique due to the Swayambu Lingam (self-manifested Lingam) of Lord Shiva, known as Vanmikanathar. The temple's presiding deity, Sri Tyagaraja Swamy, is said to have been gifted by Lord Vishnu himself, and his idol is considered to be of divine presence beyond human perception.

The temple is also home to Sri Kamalamba Devi, a powerful form of the Divine Mother, who is revered in the Sri Vidya tradition. She represents the Sahasrara Chakra, the highest level of spiritual consciousness, and is one of the Navavarana Deities in Shakti worship. Sri Neelothalamba, another powerful deity, also resides here, adding to the temple's spiritual energy.

One of the most sacred aspects of the temple is the Ajapa Natanam (Cosmic Dance of Lord Shiva), which represents the eternal rhythm of the universe and self-realization.

Maha Periyava's Stay in Thiruvarur

During his stay, Maha Periyava immersed himself in Vedantic discourses, scriptural teachings, and spiritual observances. Scholars and devotees from all over the country gathered to listen to his discourses on Advaita Vedanta and the importance of Guru Bhakti. His words, filled with deep wisdom, resonated with seekers, reinforcing their path toward self-realization and spiritual growth.

He also performed special poojas and abhishekams at the Sri Tyagaraja Swamy Temple, emphasizing the spiritual power of this sacred place. His visit revived and strengthened the devotion and faith of thousands of devotees, many of whom considered it a once-in-a-lifetime opportunity to witness the living embodiment of Sanatana Dharma.

Thiruvarur's Connection to Sundaramurthy Nayanar

Thiruvarur is closely associated with Sundaramurthy Nayanar, one of the Nalvar (Four Great Saiva Saints). He was born and lived in Thiruvarur, composing Tevaram hymns glorifying Lord Shiva. His unwavering devotion to Sri Tyagaraja Swamy led to several divine leelas (miracles), making the temple a sacred pilgrimage site for all Shaiva devotees.

Spiritual and Historical Significance of Thiruvarur

Maha Periyava highlighted the rich spiritual heritage of Thiruvarur and its immense importance in Sanatana Dharma. He explained the various aspects of the temple, including:

- The Place of Mukti (Liberation): Thiruvarur is believed to be a Mukti Sthalam, granting liberation to those who born here, worship here with pure devotion.
- The Car Festival – The Divine Car Festival: The temple hosts the grand car festival, where the deity is taken in a beautifully decorated car procession in the temple veethi.
- Connection to Sri Vidya and Navagrahas: The temple follows Sri Vidya Upasana, and Sri Kamalamba Devi's shrine is one of the most revered centers for Navavarana Pooja. The temple also has a rare Navagraha alignment, where all nine planetary deities are in a single line, making it a unique cosmic energy center.

Maha Periyava's Divine Leela at Thiruvarur

During his visit, several devotees experienced miraculous blessings from Maha Periyava. Many came to him with their problems and spiritual questions, and with his divine intuition and wisdom, he provided solutions that transformed their lives.

One such incident involved a poor devotee who was suffering from an incurable illness. Upon seeking Maha Periyava's blessings, he advised the devotee to chant the Panchakshara Mantra (Om Namah Shivaya) with complete surrender at the Sri Tyagaraja Swamy Temple. Within a short period, the devotee experienced a miraculous recovery, further affirming the divine presence of both Periyava and Lord Shiva in Thiruvarur.

Maha Periyava's Departure from Thiruvarur

After spending several days in Thiruvarur, Maha Periyava continued his yatra, moving towards other holy towns to spread the wisdom of Advaita Vedanta and Sanatana Dharma.

Maha Periyava's Divine Yatra – From Kodiyakarai to Mayavaram

Maha Periyava embarked on a sacred journey to **Kodiyakarai** (Point Calimere) during the highly auspicious Mahodaya Punyakalam to take a holy bath in the sea. Kodiyakarai is a historically and spiritually significant coastal pilgrimage site in Tamil Nadu, holding deep connections to the Ramayana. It is believed that Lord Rama, during his search for Sita Devi, offered prayers and performed rituals at this very place before crossing over to Lanka. The Mahodaya Punyakalam is considered a rare celestial alignment, and devotees who take a ritualistic bath in the sea here seek ancestral blessings, karmic cleansing, and divine grace.

Uppar Swamigal and Vedaranyam

From Kodiyakarai, Maha Periyava traveled to Vedaranyam. Vedaranyam is one of the holiest Shaivite centers, associated with Lord Shiva as Sri Vedaranyeswarar and Goddess Veena Vadha Vidhushini Amman. It is said that the four Vedas themselves worshipped Lord Vedaranyeswarar here, making it a site of profound spiritual energy.

Vedaranyam is also deeply linked to Gynanasambandar and Thirunavukkarasar (Appar) Swamigal, one of the greatest Nayanmars, who composed soul-stirring Thevaram hymns glorifying Lord Shiva at this very place.

Nagapattinam – Worship at Kayarohaneswarar Temple

From Vedaranyam, Maha Periyava proceeded to Nagapattinam and offered prayers at the Kayarohaneswarar Temple, a highly revered Shiva Kshetram. Lord Shiva is worshipped here as Kayarohaneswarar, meaning 'The Lord observing the devotees not only the soul but also with the body its do Kaya Arohana'.

The temple is associated with Sage Pundarika, who performed intense penance and was blessed by Lord Shiva. It is also believed that Goddess Parvati, in the form of Neelayadakshi (the blue-eyed goddess), performed severe austerities here to reunite with Lord Shiva. The temple is renowned for its sacred Kayarohana Theertham, a holy pond believed to have miraculous healing powers, cleansing devotees of sins and ailments. Maha Periyava's visit brought immense spiritual significance to this holy site, drawing numerous devotees eager for his darshan and blessings.

Vyasa Pooja in Mayavaram and the Revival of Vedic Studies

Following his visit to Nagapattinam, Maha Periyava reached Mayavaram (Mayiladuthurai), also known as Mayura Kshetram. According to legend, Goddess Parvati took the form of a peacock (Mayura) and performed penance here to reunite with Lord Shiva, hence the name Mayura Kshetram. The famous Mayuranathaswamy Temple stands as a testimony to this divine event, where Lord Shiva is worshipped as Mayuranathar and Goddess Abhayambikai showers her blessings upon devotees.

During his stay, Maha Periyava performed the Vyasa Pooja, In addition to spiritual discourses, Periyava took an extraordinary initiative to revive Vedic education.

Many children born into Vedic families (Vedha Parambarai) had deviated from traditional Vedic studies and adopted modern education for livelihood. To ensure that the Vedic heritage was not lost in the modern era, Maha Periyava established a special Vedic school in Rajanthottam (a garden area in Mayavaram). This initiative allowed these children to learn the Vedas during their free time and vacation, preserving the sacred tradition while adapting to changing times. His efforts rekindled interest in Vedic learning and ensured the continuation of ancient wisdom in the contemporary world.

Meeting with the Dharmapuram Adheenam

On 2nd November 1920, the Dharmapuram Adheenam, one of the most esteemed Saivite monastic institutions, visited Maha Periyava in Mayavaram. Their meeting was marked by deep discussions on Sanatana Dharma, Shaivism, and the importance of preserving temple traditions. This interaction between two great spiritual leaders further strengthened the propagation of Vedic and Shaivite traditions.

The Blind Muslim Scholar's Visit – A Testament to Periyava's Universal Grace

During his stay in Mayavaram, a blind Muslim elder, a renowned scholar in the Quran, expressed his deep desire to meet Maha Periyava. When he arrived, Periyava, instead of granting a private audience, asked him to share his wisdom with all the scholars and devotees present at the Mutt.

The Muslim scholar spoke passionately about the essence of the Quran, emphasizing love, peace, and universal brotherhood. Overwhelmed by Periyava's divine presence, he declared that Maha Periyava was a living embodiment of love and peace. With deep reverence, he proclaimed:

"I can feel the divine energy of Allah"

This profound moment reflected Maha Periyava's transcendence beyond religion, reinforcing the eternal truth that Sanatana Dharma embraces and respects all paths leading to the divine.

Legacy of Periyava's Yatra

Maha Periyava's journey was not just a pilgrimage but a **spiritual revolution**. His visit:

- **Revitalized Vedic education** through the establishment of Vedic classes.
- **Strengthened Bhakthi** through visits to historic temples.
- **Promoted religious harmony**, exemplified by his interaction with other religious scholars.
- **Inspired thousands of devotees** to follow a path of **devotion, dharma, and self-realization**.

This divine yatra continues to be **etched in history as a beacon of spiritual awakening**, guiding seekers toward the **path of truth, knowledge, and devotion**.

11

PERIYAVA'S KASI YATRA IN (1920–1921)

Visit to Sirkazhi – The Birthplace of Thirugnana Sambandar

Maha Periyava visited Vaitheeswaran Koil and then arrived at Sirkazhi (Brahmapuri), a sacred town in Tamil Nadu, revered as the birthplace of Thirugnana Sambandar, one of the great Saiva Nayanmars. The Sattainathar Temple here is unique, where Lord Shiva is worshipped in three forms—Brahmapureeswarar, Thoniappar, and Sattainathar. It is believed that Lord Shiva and Parvati fed young Sambandar divine milk, blessing him with spiritual wisdom.

Thiruvenkadu – The Abode of Budhan (Mercury)

From Sirkazhi, Periyava proceeded to Thiruvenkadu, a sacred Shaiva kshetram and a Navagraha Sthalam for Budhan (Mercury). The temple is dedicated to Swetharanyeswarar (Shiva) and Brahmavidya Nayaki, with a unique shrine for Agora Murti, a fierce form of Shiva. It is believed that sage Pattinathar and Indra worshipped here, and a holy dip in the temple's three sacred ponds grants wisdom and relief from planetary afflictions.

The Legacy of Sri Paramasivendral and Sri Sadasiva Brahmendral

Thiruvenkadu holds immense spiritual significance as the place where the 57th Peetadhipathi of Kanchi Kamakoti Peetam, Sri Paramasivendral Saraswati Swamigal, attained Siddhi. This revered Acharya was the Guru of Sri Sadasiva Brahmendral, forming a crucial link in the lineage of enlightened masters. Paramasivendral, a realized soul, upheld the Advaita tradition and guided many disciples on the path of self-realization.

Sri Sadasiva Brahmendral hailed from Thiruvisainallur, a center of scholarly excellence. Born as Sivaramakrishnan, he came to Paramasivendral to study sacred scriptures. Being an exceptional scholar, he engaged in debates with visiting scholars and consistently emerged victorious. However, his growing inclination towards intellectual superiority led to complaints from other scholars. Paramasivendral, observing this, admonished him, saying, "Can't you just remain silent?" ("Shut your mouth" in a more refined tone). Taking his Guru's words to heart, Sadasiva Brahmendral observed complete silence from that moment onward, demonstrating his absolute reverence for his Guru.

Over time, he attained yogic enlightenment, wandering in forests and villages, often unaware of his physical state. When people complained to Paramasivendral about Brahmendral's condition, Paramasivendral remarked, "I wish to attain that state of yogic realization, and he has reached it at such an early stage." This highlights the spiritual eminence of Paramasivendral, who later attained Siddhi in Thiruvenkadu.

After Paramasivendral attained Siddhi, Sadasiva Brahmendral installed his Adhishtanam and devised the pooja rituals, which continue to this day.

Periyava's Worship of Divya Desams in and Around Sirkazhi

Maha Periyava worshipped the Adhishtanam of Paramasivendral and then visited 12 Divya Desams of the Vaishnava Sampradayam around Sirkazhi. These temples, glorified in the Divya Prabandham by Azhwars, hold immense spiritual significance. The 12 Divya Desams include:

1. **Thirukazhi Cheerama Vinnagaram** – Vishnu appeared to Thirumangai Azhwar and is seen playing cymbals.
2. **Thiruvellakkulam (Annan Kovil)** – Vishnu is worshipped as Srinivasan Perumal, granting protection to devotees.
3. **Thirukkannapuram** – Home to Sowriraja Perumal, who miraculously grew long hair to fulfill a devotee's request.
4. **Thirukannangudi** – Famous for Loga Saranga Perumal and associated with Thirumangai Azhwar's service.
5. **Thirukannamangai** – Known for Bhaktavatsala Perumal, with a vast temple tank, Dharma Pushkarini.
6. **Thiruvazhundur** – Vishnu, in the form of a Brahmachari, defeated a demon here.
7. **Thiruchitrakootam (Chidambaram Govindaraja Perumal Temple)** – Vishnu and Nataraja share the divine space.
8. **Thirunagai (Nagapattinam Soundararaja Perumal Temple)** – Perumal granted moksha to Nagakannika.
9. **Thiru Indhalur (Mayavaram Parimala Ranganathar Temple)** – Vishnu in Sayana Kolam (reclining posture), relieving sins of devotees.
10. **Thiruvali Thirunagari** – Two temples known for Kalyana Ranganatha, where Thirumangai Azhwar was blessed with divine presence.
11. **Thirucherai** – Famous for Saranatha Perumal, protecting devotees as their ultimate refuge.
12. **Thirukkavalampadi** – Home to Gopalakrishna Perumal, associated with Krishna Leela.

Kaveri Poompatinam – The Sacred Sangamam

Periyava then traveled to Kaveri Poompatinam (Poompuhar), where the sacred Kaveri River merges into the ocean. According to Shastras, taking a dip at this Sangamam is highly meritorious, and Periyava undertook this divine bath.

Mahamagam and Periyava's Stay at Patteeswaram

In 1921, during the Mahamagam festival, Periyava returned to Kumbakonam but did not stay at the Mutt. Instead, he chose to stay at Patteeswaram, as he had taken a Sankalpam two years prior to not return to the Mutt until completing his Kasi Yatra. His unwavering commitment to his vows mirrored that of Lord Rama, who vowed not to enter any towns or cities during his exile.

At Patteeswaram, he visited the temple of Lord Dhenupureeswarar and worshipped Goddess Durga. The temple is renowned for the divine intervention of Lord Shiva, who instructed Nandi to step aside so that the young Thirugnana Sambandar could have a direct darshan from outside the temple. Goddess Parvati also provided him a pearl umbrella (Muthu Kudai) to shield him from the scorching sun, an event deeply etched in spiritual history.

Periyava's Initiative for Neerazhi Mandapam at Mahamagam Kulam

Periyava noticed that Mahamagam Kulam did not have a Neerazhi Mandapam, which is traditionally found in temple tanks for religious discourses and rituals. When the freedom fighter Ramabadra Udiyar visited him, Periyava expressed his desire for a mandapam to be constructed. He initiated the effort with a personal donation of Rs. 500. A small stage was built, but the full Neerazhi Mandapam remains unrealized.

Periyava's wish remains unfulfilled, and I urge the readers of this book to take up the initiative to construct the Neerazhi Mandapam at Mahamagam Kulam. Let us see who has the fortune to undertake this sacred service.

Honoring Muslim Volunteers at Mahamagam

During the Mahamagam festival, Periyava witnessed an extraordinary act of service—around 200 Muslim students from the Madras Youth Muslim Association had volunteered to help pilgrims. Moved by their selfless service, Periyava invited all 200 students to the Sri Mutt at Patteeswaram, interacted with each one personally, inquired about their families and studies, and hosted a grand feast in their honor. He presented them with silver cups in appreciation of their noble gesture.

Periyava also acknowledged the service of Congress leader Panthulu and his volunteers, inviting them for blessings and honoring their contributions.

This passage captures Periyava's unwavering commitment to Dharma, his respect for all religious communities, and his divine presence at significant sacred sites.

Maha Periyava possessed a remarkable quality—wherever he traveled, whether to temples or villages, he remained keenly observant of virtuous deeds and never hesitated to appreciate them on the spot. This trait, many say, was a hallmark of his leadership throughout his 87 years of tireless service.

Recognizing a True Patriot: The Meeting with Subramania Siva

One such instance occurred when the revered freedom fighter and ardent patriot, Sri Subramania Siva, visited Pateeswaram to seek Periyava's darshan. Though aged and afflicted with a chronic illness, Siva endured the hardships of travel for this divine meeting. Thousands had gathered to see Periyava, yet he noticed Siva standing quietly at a distance. Without hesitation, Periyava instructed his attendants to bring Siva closer. Seating him beside him, Periyava engaged in a heartfelt conversation for hours, uplifting the ailing leader's spirit.

During their discussion, Siva expressed his fervent desire for India's freedom and the nation's spiritual well-being. Periyava, with his boundless compassion, blessed him and echoed the same wish for the country's future.

A Sacred Pilgrimage: The Chaturmasya Vratham at Kathiramangalam

In 1921, Periyava observed his Chaturmasya Vratham in Kathiramangalam, home to the powerful Vana Durga Parameswari Temple. This sacred shrine, believed to have been consecrated by Sage Agastya, is known for its divine energy, where devotees seek courage, protection, and fulfillment of wishes.

After completing his Vratham, Periyava continued his yatra through Naneelam, Mayavaram, and Mannargudi, visiting numerous temples and villages along the way.

Reaching the Vathima Villages: A Testament to Tradition

During his travels, Periyava visited the eighteen Vathima villages in the Tanjore district. The Vathima community, known for its deep-rooted adherence to Vedic rituals and traditions, was blessed by his presence. These villages, thriving with prosperity and devotion, had always been significant centers of yajnas and Vedic learning.

An Unforgettable Gesture: Periyava and the Harijans of Sellur

As Periyava's grand procession made its way toward Koradacheri via Kodavasal, he passed through the village of Sellur. There, about 200 Harijans, having bathed in the river and applied vibhuti all over their bodies, eagerly awaited his arrival by the roadside. These marginalized communities, often disregarded in society, had come to seek his blessings.

The moment Periyava saw them, he ordered the palanquin to stop. Stepping down, he walked over to them, speaking to each person with genuine interest. He inquired about their livelihoods, earnings, and whether their landlords paid them fairly. He even asked about their worship practices and religious rituals.

As he spoke, Periyava mentally estimated the number of people gathered. Then, turning to his attendants, he instructed the Mutt manager to arrange dhotis and sarees for all of them. Bewildered, the manager hesitated, wondering how such a large quantity could be procured in the middle of a village road. But Periyava calmly assured him, saying, "Send a messenger to Kodavasal and arrange for it."

For the next three to four hours, as they awaited the arrival of the clothes, Periyava remained with the Harijans, giving them his undivided time and attention—an extraordinary act of compassion, especially in an era of deep social discrimination.

Meanwhile, the Mutt manager grew increasingly anxious. Periyava was scheduled to reach Koradacheri to perform the sacred Chandramouleeswarar Pooja, a ritual he never missed. Mustering courage, he reminded Periyava, "Swamigal, time is slipping away. We need to reach the camp for the Chandramouleeswarar Pooja."

Periyava, with a serene smile, replied, **"Don't you understand what I am doing now?"**

That one statement was enough to reveal the depth of his heart. For Periyava, making these Harijan devotees feel valued and uplifted was no different from performing the Chandramouleeswarar Pooja itself.

Encouraging Vedic Learning: The Stay at Poovanur

Periyava's next stop was Poovanur, where he visited Sri Raju Mudaliar's Veda Patasala, a renowned institution imparting Tamil Vedic literature, including *Thevaram* and *Thiruvasagam*. He stayed there for ten days, interacting with the students, not just listening to their recitations but also teaching them the profound meanings and significance of the verses. His presence greatly inspired them, leaving an indelible mark on their spiritual journey.

Mannargudi: The Divine Abode of Rajagopala Swamy

From Poovanur, Periyava traveled to Mannargudi, where he stayed for a month. The Mannargudi Rajagopala Swamy Temple, often called "Dakshina Dwaraka," is one of the grandest Vaishnava shrines, known for its sprawling 23-acre complex and intricate sculptures. The deity, adorned with butter and ornaments, symbolizes Lord Krishna's divine role as the protector of Dharma. The temple's *Panguni Brahmotsavam*, especially the *Garuda Seva* and *Chariot Festival*, attracts thousands of devotees.

A Fateful Event: The Passing of Sambasiva Iyer

During his stay, a devout follower, Sri Sambasiva Iyer from Kunniyur, invited Periyava to his village. Accepting the invitation, Periyava visited Kunniyur and later returned to Mannargudi. It was customary for devotees to accompany Periyava's procession to the next village or at least to the village boundary. True to tradition, Sambasiva Iyer followed him as he left.

However, midway through the journey, Periyava suddenly stopped the procession and instructed Iyer to return home immediately. Though puzzled, Iyer obeyed. By the time Periyava's procession reached Mannargudi, news arrived that Sambasiva Iyer had suffered a fatal heart attack upon reaching his home.

This was yet another instance of Periyava's divine foresight—his status as a **Trikala Jñāni (knower of past, present, and future)** was reaffirmed through countless such occurrences.

A Yatra Filled with Grace and Miracles

Periyava's journey was not just a physical pilgrimage; it was a **spiritual movement** that touched countless lives—freedom fighters, scholars, marginalized communities, and ardent devotees alike. His ability to seamlessly blend strict adherence to *Shastra* with boundless compassion made him unparalleled.

His love for humanity knew no bounds, and his yatra was filled with divine grace and miraculous moments. Many more such instances will unfold in the coming chapters.

12

MAHA PERIYAVA'S YATRA IN MADURAI AND BEYOND (1921–1923)

After completing the camp in Mannargudi, Kanchi Maha Periyava proceeded to Avudaiyarkoil, also known as Thiruperunthurai. This sacred temple holds immense spiritual significance, as it is associated with Saint Manikkavasagar, one of the four great Tamil saints and the revered author of *Tiruvachakam*. It is believed that Lord Shiva himself appeared as a Guru and initiated Manikkavasagar into divine wisdom at this very place.

Manikkavasagar, who once served as a minister in the Pandya king's court, was sent to procure horses for the royal cavalry. However, during his journey, he encountered Lord Shiva in disguise at Thiruperunthurai. Enveloped by divine grace, he used the allocated funds to construct a temple for Lord Shiva instead of purchasing the horses. When questioned by the king, Lord Shiva, in a miraculous act, transformed foxes into horses and sent them to the royal stables. However, by dawn, the foxes reverted to their original form, enraging the king, who then imprisoned Manikkavasagar. To demonstrate the power of devotion, Lord Shiva caused the Vaigai River to flood. When the king ordered every citizen to contribute to controlling the flood, Shiva appeared as a laborer and deliberately delayed the work, leading the king to recognize the divine intervention. Understanding Manikkavasagar's unwavering devotion, the king freed him. Manikkavasagar then renounced worldly life, composed *Tiruvachakam*, and became one of the 63 Nayanmars, eternally venerated for his deep devotion and poetic hymns.

The Avudaiyarkoil temple, where Periyava worshipped Lord Shiva, is a marvel of spiritual and architectural grandeur. Unlike conventional Shiva temples, this shrine has no Lingam in the sanctum; instead, the Avudaiyar (base of the Lingam) is worshipped, symbolizing the formless nature of Shiva (*Nirguna Brahman*). The temple is adorned with breathtaking stone carvings—sculpted chains, ceiling fans, and lifelike floral motifs—all testifying to the Chola-era sculptors' unparalleled artistry. The temple's pillars and ceilings are richly decorated with celestial beings, sages, and intricate mythological depictions, bringing to life various divine narratives. Here, Manikkavasagar is portrayed in deep meditation, emphasizing his profound spiritual connection with Lord Shiva. Every sculptural element carries deep symbolism, illustrating devotion, divine grace, and self-realization.

During his visit to Avudaiyarkoil, Periyava performed the *Vishwaroopa Pooja* in the presence of the Thiruvavaduthurai Aadheenam. The revered Katalaithambiran Swamigal performed *Bikshavandanam* and *Padha Pooja* for Periyava, reinforcing the sacred guru-disciple tradition and the philosophical essence of Advaita Vedanta. This gathering was a profound testimony to the eternal connection between *Jnana* (spiritual wisdom) and *Bhakti* (devotion).

From Avudaiyarkoil, Periyava continued his divine journey, visiting various temples and villages, including Uppur, where he worshipped Maha Ganapathi, installed by Sri Rama, and Devipattinam, also known as Nava Pashanam. He then reached Rameshwaram, a sacred *Jyotirlinga* site and an essential destination in the Char Dham Yatra. It is here that Lord Rama is believed to have worshipped Shiva to atone for any sins incurred during his battle with Ravana. The Ramanathaswamy Temple is renowned for its 22 *Theerthams* (sacred wells), where devotees take ritual baths for spiritual purification. The temple's corridors, the longest among Hindu temples, are a true architectural wonder. A pilgrimage to Rameshwaram is considered complete only after a dip in the sea and performing puja at this sanctified site, marking the culmination of a *Kasi Yatra*.

As Periyava walked towards Rameshwaram, there was no road bridge connecting the mainland to Pamban in those days. Since Periyava never used vehicles, he chose to walk across the Pamban rail bridge, carrying Chandramouleeswarar. The *Mutt* sought and received permission from the British authorities for this sacred journey. Meanwhile, the other devotees of the *Mutt* traveled by boat to Pamban, an arrangement facilitated by the devout Marakayar of Mandapam.

Periyava, upon arriving in Rameshwaram, performed ritual baths in the sacred *Theerthams*, including Agni Theertham, believed to be the very spot where Lord Rama conducted rituals for Lord Shiva. Each *Theertham* is associated with divine legends, sages, and spiritual purification. Devotees traditionally bathe in a prescribed sequence, culminating in worship at the Ramanathaswamy Temple.

From Rameshwaram, Periyava proceeded to Dhanushkodi, where he performed the *Navaratri Pooja*. On the *Puratasi Purnima* (Full Moon Day) of 1922, he collected sand from Dhanushkodi to be ceremoniously offered at Prayag, embarking on his journey to Kashi. Before departing, Periyava performed a grand *Dhanam* (charity), distributing wealth worth ₹10,000 to Pandits—a sum equivalent to millions today.

During his stay in Dhanushkodi, Mahatma Gandhi had launched the *Khadi Movement*, promoting the use of handspun cloth. Periyava, moved by the cause, resolved to wear only *Khadi* for the rest of his life. He instructed the *Mutt* disciples to procure 200 *Khadi* garments from Madurai for the entire group, remaining committed to the cause even after India gained independence.

One day, as Periyava was returning from a ritual sea bath, he encountered a gathering of beggars. While distributing alms, an elderly beggar stepped forward. A wealthy man, irritated by the beggar's presence, struck him with a walking stick, causing him to bleed. Deeply affected by the incident, Periyava sternly reprimanded the rich man, teaching him the virtue of *Shanthi* (peace). He instructed the *Mutt* manager to take the injured beggar to a hospital. The remorseful landlord sought forgiveness and pledged to renounce his anger, embracing humility and kindness.

On October 10, 1922, Periyava arrived in Ramanathapuram, where he was warmly welcomed by Raja Muthuramalinga Sethupathi. The king requested Periyava to stay in his palace, where he remained for six days, spreading spiritual wisdom and reinforcing the traditions of *Sanatana Dharma*.

Periyava continued his yatra, traveling from Manamadurai to Sivagangai. The ruler of Sivagangai extended an invitation, and Periyava stayed there for five days before proceeding to Kalayarkoil. He then visited Thiruvadhavoor and arrived at the sacred town of Thirukoshtiyur.

Thirukoshtiyur: A Sacred Vaishnavite Pilgrimage

Thirukoshtiyur, a revered Divya Desam near Sivagangai, holds immense spiritual and historical significance for Vaishnavites. The Thirukoshtiyur Perumal Temple, dedicated to Sri Sowmya Narayana Perumal, is particularly renowned as the site where the great Vaishnavite saint Sri Ramanujacharya received the sacred Ashtakshara Mantra ("Om Namo Narayanaya") from his guru, Thirukoshtiyur Nambi. In an act of supreme compassion, Sri Ramanuja defied the instruction to keep the mantra secret and instead proclaimed it from the temple tower for the benefit of all, earning him the revered title of *Emperumaanar*.

The temple structure is unique, designed with five tiers representing the *Pancha Koshas* (five sheaths of the human body). The presiding deity, Sri Sowmya Narayana Perumal, is enshrined in three distinct postures—*Nindra* (standing), *Irundha* (sitting), and *Kidantha* (reclining)—a rare feature among Divya Desams. The Goddess, Thirumamagal Nachiyar (Mahalakshmi), blesses devotees alongside Perumal. A significant shrine dedicated to Lord Narasimha further elevates the temple's sanctity.

The name *Thirukoshtiyur* originates from the Sanskrit word *Koshthi*, meaning "assembly" or "gathering." Legend has it that celestial beings (*Devas*) assembled here to seek Lord Vishnu's intervention in defeating the demon Hiranyakashipu. Lord Narasimha manifested here, assuring them of divine protection, thus giving the town its sacred name.

As one of the 108 Divya Desams glorified in the *Divya Prabandham* by Alwars, particularly Tirumangai Alwar, Thirukoshtiyur remains a key landmark in Vaishnavite tradition. The temple's towering *Ashtanga Vimana*, where Sri Ramanuja preached the *Ashtakshara Mantra*, continues to be a beacon of Bhakti and divine wisdom.

Periyava continued his spiritual journey across Tamil Nadu, visiting numerous holy sites en route to Kashi. He traveled through Thirupattur, Elayathankudi, Pranmalai, Azhagar Kovil, and Pazhamuthircholai, finally arriving in Madurai on **November 12, 1922**.

Periyava's Grand Welcome in Madurai

The people of Madurai received Periyava with great reverence and celebration. His presence turned the city into a festival of devotion, and he remained in Madurai for a month.

From Madurai, Periyava proceeded to **Srivilliputtur**, one of the holiest Vaishnavite pilgrimage sites.

Srivilliputtur: The Abode of Andal

Srivilliputtur is deeply revered for its association with Andal, the only female Alwar and an incarnation of Goddess Bhudevi. The **Srivilliputtur Andal Temple** enshrines Andal alongside Sri Vatapatrasayi Perumal (Lord Vishnu). According to legend, Andal was discovered as a divine child in the temple garden by Periyalwar, a devoted saint. Immersed in unwavering Bhakti, she composed the *Tiruppavai* and *Nachiyar Thirumozhi*, which remain timeless hymns of devotion. Andal's mystical union with Lord Ranganatha at Srirangam cements her legacy as the divine consort of Vishnu.

The temple's towering Rajagopuram, an architectural marvel, is the official emblem of the Tamil Nadu government. Srivilliputtur continues to draw devotees seeking Andal's grace and spiritual enlightenment.

Periyava's journey then took him through Kadayanallur, Tenkasi, Kadayam, and Papanasam, reaching Tirunelveli in January 1923. From there, he visited Alwarthirunagari, Srivaikuntam, and Nanguneri, finally arriving in Tiruchendur on February 11, 1923.

Tiruchendur: The Sacred Seaside Abode of Lord Muruga

Tiruchendur, one of the *Arupadai Veedu* (six sacred abodes) of Lord Muruga, is unique as it stands majestically along the shores of the Bay of Bengal, unlike other hilltop Murugan temples. According to legend, after defeating the demon Surapadman, Lord Muruga worshipped Lord Shiva here in gratitude, sanctifying the site. The grand Skanda Shasti festival reenacts this celestial battle, drawing lakhs of devotees.

The temple's architectural grandeur includes the Shanmuga Vilasa Mandapam, a towering nine-tier Rajagopuram, and the revered Nazhikkinaru well, whose freshwater spring near the sea is believed to have miraculous healing powers.

Adi Shankaracharya himself extolled the sanctity of the Vibhuti Prasadam offered in *Panneer* leaves at Tiruchendur, emphasizing its divine fragrance and spiritual potency. Periyava stayed here for five days before continuing his journey.

Thirukuttralam: The Sacred Dance Hall of Lord Nataraja

Periyava then reached Thirukuttralam, home to the Chitra Sabha, one of Lord Nataraja's Pancha Sabhas (*Five Cosmic Dance Halls*). Unlike the grand stone structures of the other Sabhas, the Chitra Sabha is a beautifully painted wooden hall, adorned with intricate murals depicting celestial beings and divine events.

It is believed that Lord Shiva performed his Ananda Tandavam (Cosmic Dance) here to bless devotees. The sacred Courtallam waterfalls, near the temple, are believed to purify and grant liberation to those who bathe in them.

After offering prayers at Thirukuttralam, Periyava traveled to Kallidaikurichi, where he stayed for a week, receiving immense devotion from the local villagers. He then continued his journey through Kovilpatti and Sattur, reaching Dindigul, where he stayed for three days.

Periyava's Tapas at Sirumalai

From Dindigul, Periyava undertook an arduous journey to Sirumalai, accompanied by only a few Mutt devotees. He climbed the hill and engaged in deep *Tapas* (meditative penance) at the summit. The security and arrangements for this sacred retreat were overseen by the Kanniwadi Zamindar.

Palani: The Abode of Lord Dhandayuthapani

After completing his penance, Periyava traveled to Palani, one of the *Arupadai Veedu* of Lord Murugan. Perched atop Sivagiri Hill, the Palani Murugan Temple enshrines Lord Dhandayuthapani in an ascetic form, embodying renunciation and devotion.

Thirumayam: A Devotee's Offering

During his visit to Thirumayam, Sri Muthiah Chettiar, a devoted follower, offered a **gold plate** for Periyava's Pooja. This sacred plate remains preserved at the Mutt to this day, a testament to the unwavering devotion Periyava inspired in his followers.

ॐ

13

MAHA PERIYAVA'S VISIT TO NERUR AND BEYOND (1923–1924)

Periyava's Journey from Thirumayam to Thiruvanaikoil

In 1923, Periyava continued his spiritual yatra from Thirumayam to Pudukkottai, where the government received him with great honor and performed the Sahasra Padha Pooja. From there, Periyava proceeded to Thiruvanaikoil, a place of immense spiritual significance.

As mentioned in the fourth chapter of this book, Thiruvanaikoil holds a special place in the history of the Kanchi Mutt, despite the Mutt having several branches across India. One of the most significant branches of the Kanchi Mutt is located here.

During his stay at the Thiruvanaikoil Mutt, the Upanayanam ceremony of the renowned scientist Sir M. Visvesvaraya was performed, as recorded in his writings.

Thadanga Pratishta and the Grand Astika Maanadu

On 29th April 1923, the Thadanga Pratishta was performed in Thiruvanaikoil. As discussed earlier in the fourth chapter, this ritual was originally installed by Adi Shankaracharya, and it is a sacred tradition for the Kanchi Shankaracharya to perform this ceremony once every twelve years.

This year, during the Thadanga Pratishta, Periyava arranged for a grand Astika Maanadu (public conference on theism), which was meticulously organized by T.K. Balasubramaniyar, the owner of Srirangam Vanivilas Press. The event was conducted on a grand scale, attracting massive participation.

T.K. Balasubramaniyar, who also ran a journal called *The Hindu Message*, published a detailed editorial on 10th May 1923 about the event. He wrote:

"Never before has Trichy witnessed such a grand Thadanga Pratishta. The procession of devotees stretched for more than a mile. The streets were decorated extensively, and it took five hours for the procession to cross a single location. No king, British ruler, or political leader in India has ever received such a grand welcome. This event was unparalleled in scale and devotion."

Visit to Nerur and Meditation at Sadasiva Brahmendral's Adhishtanam

After completing the Thadanga Pratishta at Thiruvanaikoil, Periyava continued his yatra through Kuzhithalai, Krishnarajapuram, Mahadhanapuram, Karur, and reached Nerur—the site of the Adhishtanam of Sadasiva Brahmendral.

At the Adhishtanam, there is a massive Vilva tree (Bael tree), which is sacred to Lord Shiva. In front of the tree stands a Lingam that was brought from Kashi. As discussed in an earlier chapter, Sri Sadasiva Brahmendral was the disciple of Paramasiva Brahmendral, the 57th Acharya of the Kanchi Kamakoti Peetam.

Maha Periyava spent several hours meditating in front of the Adhishtanam, as this place was very close to his heart.

Preventing Religious Conversions

In June 1923, from Nerur, Periyava traveled to Kulumani, where he met Sri F.G. Natesa Iyer, the Trichy Municipal Chairman. Natesa Iyer brought along a Kerala Brahmin, who was considering converting to another religion due to certain influences. Since Natesa Iyer himself had embraced Christianity for some time before returning to Hinduism, he advised the young man on the significance of Hinduism and its spiritual richness. However, he felt that only Periyava could provide true clarity.

At Natesa Iyer's request, Periyava asked the man to stay in the Mutt for two days. After speaking to him about Hindu philosophy and traditions, the young man was convinced and decided not to convert.

Another such case involved a man named Venkataramani from Vellore, who had studied in a Christian missionary school. He believed that only Christianity promoted service and intended to convert, much to his parents' sorrow. As a last request, his parents urged him to meet Maha Periyava before making his final decision.

While he stood in the crowd awaiting Periyava's darshan, a foreign lady approached Periyava, expressing her deep admiration for Hinduism and her wish to convert. However, Periyava advised:

"All religions teach peace and service to mankind. Every faith provides a path to attain purity and moksha. There is no need to convert from one religion to another. You can stay in your own faith and still serve humanity."

He further explained

"The other side always appears greener. Just like mountains in the distance seem smaller while the nearest ones appear larger, we tend to perceive what is close to us as significant and undervalue what is distant. We must remove such illusions from our minds."

Hearing this profound wisdom, Venkataramani understood the value of Hinduism and decided to remain in his faith. He returned home, fell at his parents' feet, and abandoned the idea of conversion.

A Mother's Grief and Periyava's Compassion

One day, a grief-stricken lady visited Periyava's Mutt, having lost her young son in an accident. She wept at Periyava's feet, fearing that her son's soul might be wandering in unrest. She asked if any pooja or rituals could be performed to ensure her son attained peace.

Periyava, deeply moved, had tears in his eyes. He gently told her:

"No need for elaborate rituals or poojas. Just ensure that every day, you serve buttermilk and fresh drinking water to the workers in your paddy fields and gardens. Let them stay hydrated in the scorching sun. This act of kindness will bring peace to your son's soul."

The woman was comforted but felt guilty for having made Periyava cry. Periyava reassured her:

"Do not replace one sorrow with another. You were grieving for your son; now that you are relieved, do not start another sorrow by worrying about me. Understand that Periyava has no personal emotions or attachments. What you saw was simply the Dharma of a true Sadhu."

Periyava's Role in the Hindu Dharmastabana Masoda

During Periyava's stay in Trichy in 1923, a crucial event took place. The Justice Party, led by Panagal Raja, introduced a draft bill called the Hindu Dharmastabana Masoda, aimed at protecting Hindu temples and religious institutions. The government sought feedback from the public and religious leaders.

Periyava convened a discussion with experienced lawyers and scholars to analyze the draft. He suggested key amendments to rectify sections that compromised the bill's core purpose.

Periyava entrusted **Mahalinga Iyer** to present these changes to Panagal Raja. Upon receiving Periyava's feedback, Panagal Raja personally convened a **committee at St. George Fort**. In the final meeting, **T.R. Ramachandra Iyer** advocated for the corrections, leading to the bill's improvement. Panagal Raja publicly expressed gratitude to Periyava for his invaluable contributions.

Sacred Renovation of Kudanthai Keezhkottam Nageswaraswamy Temple

In June 1923, in Kumbakonam, Kudanthai Keezhkottam, stands the temple dedicated to Lord Shiva. This temple holds immense spiritual and astrological significance, particularly for devotees seeking relief from Rahu dosha in their horoscopes. It is one of the important temples associated with Rahu Bhagavan.

According to legend, this temple is linked to the celestial event of Samudra Manthan (churning of the ocean), where Lord Shiva consumed the deadly poison (Halahala) to save the universe. After swallowing the poison, Shiva's throat turned blue, and to alleviate its effects, he rested here. This temple is also famous for its unique worship practices related to Navagraha Rahu Bhagavan, where devotees perform special poojas to remove obstacles, reduce planetary afflictions, and gain prosperity.

During this time, Sri Padagacherry Swamigal dedicated himself to arranging the Kumbhabhishekham (consecration ceremony). He devoted his life to this noble cause, tying a pot around his neck and walking through the streets of Kumbakonam, collecting donations in cash and kind to build the Raja Gopuram of this temple. Remarkably, he never directly asked for money or donations; he simply walked, and people contributed whatever they could.

Resolving the Dispute Over Kumbhabhishekham

When the temple renovation was complete, Padagacherry Swamigal set a date for the Kumbhabhishekham. However, a dispute arose between the Sthapathis (craftsmen) and the temple priests over who should perform the Abhishekam to the Kalasam first. The matter escalated and reached the court.

Padagacherry Swamigal sought the guidance of Maha Periyava to resolve this issue. Periyava requested both parties to meet him to discuss the matter. Padagacherry Swamigal convinced them to accept Periyava's decision as final.

Periyava, following the Sastras, ruled that the Sthapathis should perform the Abhishekam first, as guided in the scriptures, followed by the temple priests (Shivacharyas). Both parties amicably agreed, and the Kumbhabhishekham was successfully conducted in June 1923. This incident occurred while Periyava was in Trichy.

Periyava's Yatra to Thiruvaiyaru

In 1924, Periyava continued his yatra to Thiruvaiyaru and performed the Vyasa Pooja there. The presiding deity of Thiruvaiyaru Temple is Sri Ayyarappar (Panchanadeeswarar), a form of Lord Shiva, and the Goddess is Sri Dharmasamvardhini Amman. Lord Ayyarappar is revered as the divine protector of dharma, and the temple is one of the Padal Petra Sthalams mentioned in the Thevaram hymns.

Thiruvaiyaru, meaning "the land of five rivers," is home to the Sri Ayyarappar Temple, which has deep spiritual and historical significance. The temple is celebrated for its grand Panchanadeeswarar shrine, reflecting Chola architecture with majestic pillars, intricate sculptures, and inscriptions that highlight its centuries-old history. This place is also known for its association with Saint Thyagaraja, one of the greatest Carnatic composers, whose annual aradhana is held here.

The Great Flood of 1924 and Periyava's Divine Protection

Following the Vyasa Pooja, Periyava commenced the Chaturmasyam Pooja. Chaturmasyam falls during the rainy season, and in 1924, there were heavy rains followed by a massive flood. The rivers Cauvery and Kollidam, which are three kilometers apart, merged due to the flooding, submerging the land between them completely.

Periyava was staying on the banks of the Cauvery during this period. The townspeople were deeply concerned about his safety, as the rising waters posed a grave threat. However, as a staunch follower of dharma and tradition, Periyava refused to move. According to the rules of Chaturmasyam, once the pooja began, he was bound to remain in the same place for four months. His unwavering faith amazed the villagers, but they also feared for his safety.

Miraculously, the water did not rise near the spot where Periyava was staying, though the surrounding villages were completely submerged. Recognizing the dire situation, Periyava arranged for Annadhanam (food distribution) for all the affected villagers. The Mutt devotees cooked food, which was transported by elephants and boats to reach those stranded by the flood. The government was unable to provide aid, but Periyava and his devotees served the villagers tirelessly for 15 days until the waters receded.

After the flood subsided, the Collector of Tanjore, H.M. Hood, personally visited Periyava to express his gratitude for saving the villagers.

Periyava's Act of Divine Protection – Reminiscent of Lord Krishna

Periyava's actions during the flood were likened to Lord Krishna's divine act of lifting the Govardhan Hill to protect the people of Gokulam from torrential rains sent by Indra. In a similar manner, Periyava shielded the villagers from suffering and provided them with food and relief when no other help was available.

Rebuilding Kallar Street After a Devastating Fire

Another incident highlighting Periyava's compassion occurred in Kumbakonam's Kallar Street. A massive fire engulfed the entire street, destroying homes and leaving families destitute. In response, Periyava ordered the Mutt to reconstruct all the houses and provide the affected families with new belongings. His kindness and selfless service to humanity stood as a testament to his divine grace and unwavering commitment to the welfare of the people.

14

Maha Periyava's Yatra in Vallam & Elayathangudi (1924–1925)

Maha Periyava's Forethought: Protecting People from Disasters

1924 Floods: Periyava's Compassion in Action

We have already seen how Maha Periyava safeguarded people during the devastating floods in Thiruvaiyaru in 1924. This act of compassion was not an isolated event—it was a testament to Periyava's divine foresight and his unwavering commitment to serving humanity.

This reminds us of an earlier incident that occurred in 1914, during a catastrophic flood in Bengal's Gulna region, which left thousands dead, homeless, and destitute. The calamity triggered a nationwide relief movement, with volunteers from across India stepping forward to help.

A Historic Contribution: The Kanchi Mutt's Relief Efforts

During this crisis, Sri Kasturiranga Iyengar, the owner of *The Hindu* newspaper, initiated a large-scale campaign to collect relief materials. He published an appeal, urging people to donate generously.

When Maha Periyava saw the appeal, he immediately instructed the Kanchi Mutt Manager to donate ₹500, a staggering amount in those days, equivalent to several lakhs in today's value. The Mutt promptly sent a telegram money order to *The Hindu*.

Upon receiving the donation, Kasturiranga Iyengar was left speechless. It was unprecedented for a Mathathipathi to contribute directly to a social cause. Overwhelmed by Periyava's compassion, he wrote a heartfelt letter of gratitude, acknowledging that this was the first-ever relief contribution from a religious Mutt in India.

Later, when Maha Periyava visited Chennai, he visited *The Hindu* office and personally blessed Kasturiranga Iyengar and his team for their noble work.

This recaps the 1964 Rameshwaram Cyclone and Periyava's Divine Foresight

Fifty years later, in 1964, another natural disaster struck—this time in Rameshwaram. The infamous cyclone completely wiped out Dhanushkodi, leaving the region cut off from the mainland and its people stranded without food or shelter.

But months before the cyclone struck, Periyava had already foreseen the impending disaster.

The Mysterious Order: Gathering Grains for an Unknown Purpose

From 1963 onwards, Maha Periyava began requesting cultivators and farmers to donate a sack of paddy each to the Kanchi Mutt. This was highly unusual, as Periyava never sought donations for the Mutt's sustenance.

The collected paddy sacks were then sent to the Rameshwaram Mutt. Within weeks, the Mutt's storehouses were overflowing. The

Rameshwaram Mutt Manager, Vishwanatha Iyer, confused by the sudden influx of grain, repeatedly wrote to Kanchi Mutt seeking clarification.

Despite multiple letters, no reply came from Kanchi Mutt or Periyava. Frustrated, Vishwanatha Iyer decided to travel to Kanchipuram to seek answers directly from Periyava.

The Divine Silence: When Periyava Speaks Through Actions

Upon reaching Kanchi Mutt, he met the manager, who admitted that even he had no explanation. Every inquiry about the grain had been met with silence from Periyava.

When Vishwanatha Iyer finally approached Periyava, he asked, *"Why have you sent so many paddy sacks to Rameshwaram when there are so few devotees there? Should we distribute it elsewhere?"*

Periyava simply smiled and replied, *"I did not ask for our usage here."*

Confused, the manager suggested donating the paddy to Ramanatha Swamy Temple. Again, Periyava only smiled and remained silent.

Finally, exasperated, the Kanchi Mutt Manager told Vishwanatha Iyer, *"If you don't have space to store the grains, just throw them into the ocean!"*

Periyava did not respond. Instead, he simply went inside his room.

The Cyclone Strikes: Periyava's Grains Become Lifesaving Food

Soon after Vishwanatha Iyer returned to Rameshwaram, the 1964 cyclone struck. The entire town was devastated, cutting off all access to the mainland. Food supplies ran out, and people were on the brink of starvation.

At that moment, Periyava dispatched devotees from Kanchi Mutt to Rameshwaram. Battling storms and difficult terrain, these devotees reached just before the land connection was completely severed.

Periyava instructed them to grind the stored paddy into rice, cook food, and serve Annadanam to the affected people.

For weeks, the Mutt's collected paddy sustained the entire population of Rameshwaram, saving thousands from starvation. Only then did the Mutt managers realize why Periyava had collected and stored the grains in advance.

This divine foresight once again confirmed that **Maha Periyava was a Trikala Jñāni**—one who knows the past, present, and future.

Why Periyava Never Explained His Actions

Despite numerous inquiries, Periyava never revealed the reason for his actions beforehand. This is the true quality of a Mahan—they act selflessly for the benefit of humanity without seeking recognition or explanation.

As he often said, *"A leader does not need to explain everything. When the time comes, the truth will reveal itself."*

Continuing the Yatra: Periyava's Visit to Varahur and Vallam

After the 1924 floods, Maha Periyava continued his yatra towards Thirukattupalli, where he stayed at a school established by P.S. Sivaswamy Iyer.

He then traveled through Nemam, Pazhamaneri, Ombathuveli, Ranganathapuram, and finally reached Varahur, home to the Varahur Varadaraja Perumal Temple.

Varahur: A Sacred Musical and Spiritual Heritage

Varahur is revered as a Divya Desam Kshetram, closely associated with Saint Thyagaraja and Narayana Theerthar, the composer of *Sri Krishna Leela Tarangini*.

The great sage Narayana Theerthar once suffered from an ailment and prayed at this temple. By taking a holy dip in the sacred theertham, he was miraculously cured, leading him to compose some of his most profound devotional songs in praise of Lord Vishnu.

Even today, Varahur is a pilgrimage site for musicians and devotees, who seek divine blessings for artistic excellence and spiritual upliftment. Famous Uriyadi Utsavam during Janmashtami.

A Grand Welcome in Vallam

After visiting Varahur, Periyava proceeded to **Vallam**, where he received an **unprecedented welcome**. People from all religious backgrounds gathered in large numbers to witness and celebrate his arrival.

Periyava's yatra then took him to **Pudukottai**, marking yet another milestone in his divine journey.

Maha Periyava and Tamil Literature: The Felicitation of U.V. Swaminatha Iyer

One of the most significant events organized by Maha Periyava was the grand felicitation of U.V. Swaminatha Iyer, the legendary Tamil scholar known as Tamizh Thatha (Grandfather of Tamil).

Periyava, recognizing his contributions to reviving ancient Tamil literature, ensured that the event was conducted with the utmost reverence. Swaminatha Iyer, in turn, hailed Maha Periyava as "Tamil Deivam".

The Parampara of Chandramouleeswara Pooja

U.V. Swaminatha Iyer recalled witnessing Ilayathangudi Periyava's Chandramouleeswara Pooja in his youth. He was amazed at how Periyava could identify and discard imperfect Vilva leaves without even opening his eyes. Decades later, he saw the same perfection in Maha Periyava's Chandramouleeswara Pooja, proving the unbroken spiritual lineage of Kanchi Kamakoti Peetam.

The Eternal Wisdom of Maha Periyava

From orchestrating relief efforts to preserving Tamil heritage and spiritual traditions, Maha Periyava's life continues to inspire generations. His divine foresight, unwavering compassion, and silent miracles reaffirm his role as one of the greatest spiritual luminaries of our time.

The Divine Legacy of the Chandramouleeswara Lingam

The Chandramouleeswara Lingam, worshipped daily at the Kanchi Kamakoti Peetam, holds profound spiritual significance as it was bestowed upon Adi Shankaracharya by Lord Shiva himself. According to tradition, when Adi Shankara embarked on his divine mission to re-establish Sanatana Dharma across Bharat, Lord Shiva, pleased with his devotion and wisdom, in his infinite grace, gifted him five sacred Chandramouleeswara Lingams, each imbued with divine energy. These Lingams, representing Lord Shiva in his cosmic form with the crescent moon adorning his locks, were meant for his personal worship and the propagation of Advaita Vedanta.

Adi Shankara is believed to have performed intense Abhisheka and Pooja to these Lingams, invoking Shiva's divine presence and blessings. The Kanchi Acharyas have continued this unbroken tradition of worship, offering sacred Rudrabhishekam and Archana to the Chandramouleeswara Lingam thrice a day, ensuring that its divine vibrations continue to bless devotees. This Lingam remains a symbol of spiritual continuity, reinforcing the divine connection between Adi Shankaracharya, Lord Shiva, and the Kanchi Kamakoti Peetam.

The Five Chandramouleeswara Lingams and Their Sacred Locations

Adi Shankaracharya installed the **five Chandramouleeswara Lingams** in the following sacred locations, which later became the **Shankaracharya Peethams**:

1. **Sringeri Sharada Peetham – Karnataka**

   o The first Bhoga Lingam among the Peethams, Sringeri near the confluence of the Tunga and Bhadra rivers. houses the Chandramouleeswara Lingam, worshipped daily with great devotion. This Lingam is the principal deity of the Peetham, and Adi Shankara himself established the tradition of worship here.

2. **Kanchipuram Kanchi Kamakoti Peetham – Tamil Nadu**

   o Kanchipuram, another significant spiritual center, enshrines a Yoga Lingam/Chandramouleeswara Lingam, where the pontiffs of this Peetham continue the unbroken tradition of Shiva worship as prescribed by the Acharya.

3. **Vara Lingam – Nepal**

   o Adi Shankara installed one of the sacred Pancha Chandramouleeswara Lingams, is also venerated as a powerful Neelakandeshwar Kshetram Located in the Himalayas, the Vara Lingam draws seekers and sadhakas who come to perform intense worship and meditation, considering it a potent center of purification, tapas, and liberation.

4. **Mukthi Lingam – Kedarnath**

   o   Nestled in the Himalayas at an altitude of over 11,000 feet, Kedarnath is not only one of the twelve Jyotirlingas but also a spiritual powerhouse where Lord Shiva is worshipped as the granter of ultimate freedom from the cycle of birth and death. The Chandramouleeswara aspect here emphasizes the **cosmic form of Shiva adorned with the crescent moon**, radiating grace and transcendence, making the Mukthi Lingam a magnet for pilgrims and sages seeking spiritual release and union with the Divine.

5. **Moksha Lingam – Chidambaram**

   o   Nestled within the **Thillai Nataraja Temple**, this sacred lingam represents Lord Shiva as the cosmic dancer who reveals the truth behind creation, sustenance, and dissolution. Unlike other shrines, Chidambaram is unique for its worship of both the **form (lingam)** and the **formless (Chidambara Rahasyam)** aspects of the Divine, signifying the transcendence of duality. The Chandramouleeswara aspect here symbolizes Shiva's boundless compassion, crowned by the crescent moon, bestowing knowledge and liberation upon earnest seekers who come to this hallowed ground.

Each of these places continues to follow the sacred Shiva Puja rituals set by Adi Shankara, maintaining the spiritual essence of Sanatana Dharma and upholding the Advaita Vedanta philosophy.

The Revelation of Soundaryalahari

Along with these sacred Lingams, Lord Shiva also revealed to Adi Shankara the Soundaryalahari, a celestial hymn extolling the divine beauty and power of Devi Parvati. As Adi Shankara descended from Mount Kailash, carrying this hymn, Nandi Deva, the devoted mount of Shiva, intercepted him, declaring that such a powerful text was not meant for the world. In a moment of divine intervention, Nandi snatched the manuscript, tearing away a portion of it. As a result, Adi Shankara was left with only 41 verses, which constitute the first part of Soundaryalahari, while the remaining 59 verses were later revealed to him through divine vision.

This sacred text remains a cornerstone of Shakta worship, glorifying Sri Lalita Tripurasundari and containing potent mantras and yantras for spiritual elevation. Just as the five Chandramouleeswara Lingams continue to radiate divine energy, the Soundaryalahari remains an unparalleled spiritual treatise, eternally resonating with Shiva-Shakti's boundless grace.

Maha Periyava and the Chandramouleeswara Pooja

When Maha Periyava ascended the Acharya Peetam at the age of 13, the Sastrigals began teaching him the rituals of performing the Chandramouleeswara Pooja. They instructed him that when performing the Chandramouleeswara Pooja, he should have the bhavam (feeling) that he and Chandramouleeswara are one and the same. Though the ritual follows a Dvaitic approach, one should uphold the Advaitic realization.

As expressed in the sacred verse

- **"Deho Devalayaḥ proktaḥ, Jīvo Devaḥ sanātanaḥ I Tyajedajñāna-nirmālyaṁ, So'ham bhāvena pūjayet II"**
- **Deho Devalayaḥ proktaḥ** – The body is said to be a **temple**.

- **Jīvo Devaḥ sanātanaḥ** – The **soul (Jīva)** is the **eternal deity residing within**.
- **Tyajedajñāna-nirmālyaṁ** – One must **remove the impurity of ignorance**.
- **So'ham bhāvena pūjayet** – And **worship with the realization of "I am That" (So'ham)**.

Significance:

This verse emphasizes the Advaita Vedanta philosophy that the body itself is a temple, and the soul within is none other than the divine. Instead of merely engaging in external rituals, one must recognize the divinity within, discard ignorance, and worship through self-realization. It encourages seekers to cultivate inner purity and perceive themselves as one with the Supreme.

Maha Periyava's Divine Response

Upon hearing this explanation, Maha Periyava posed a **profound question**: *"Should we have this Bhavam only when performing the pooja? Or should we have this Bhavam always?"*

Realizing the depth of his understanding, the Sastrigals immediately recognized that they were speaking to Maha Periyava himself and apologized for their limited perspective.

The Historic Chaturmasya of Two Acharyas in 1925

In 1925, Maha Periyava continued his yatra to Elayathangudi and performed Chaturmasya Pooja. At the same time, Sringeri Shankaracharya Sri Chandrasekarendra Bharathi was in Kunnakudi, just 5 kilometers away, performing his own Chaturmasya Pooja.

This rare occasion brought immense joy to the people, who were blessed to have darshan of both the Acharyas within such close proximity. The two Peethathipathis, revered spiritual giants, stayed in the same region, offering their blessings to countless devotees, marking an event of great spiritual significance in modern history.

These divine episodes not only reinforce the legacy of Adi Shankaracharya but also highlight Maha Periyava's profound spiritual wisdom, upholding the eternal truth of Advaita Vedanta through the Chandramouleeswara Pooja and the unbroken lineage of the Acharyas.

The Journey Continues

In 1925, after completing the Chaturmasya pooja at Elayathangudi, Maha Periyava resumed his yatra towards Kanadukathan. Upon his arrival, Sir M.C.T. Muthiah Chettiar accorded him a grand reception and earnestly requested him to stay for a while. Honoring the request, Periyava remained in Kanadukathan for 15 days, blessing the town and its people with his divine presence.

From there, Periyava continued his journey to Kariapatti, where he bestowed the title of "Dharma Bhushanam" upon TN. Muthiah Chettiar, recognizing his family's immense contributions to dharma karya. Their generous efforts included the renovation of the Cuddalore Thirupathiripuliyur Padaleeswarar Temple and the donation of a silver chariot to the Thiruvannamalai Annamalaiyar Temple.

The Devotion of Ramanathan Chettiar

During Periyava's stay in Kariapatti, many scholars came for his darshan. Among them was Ramanathan Chettiar, a renowned Tamil scholar. He spent a week at the Mutt, engaging in deep discussions with Periyava about Tamil literature.

One day, the Nagarathars of Karaikudi organized a grand procession in Kariapatti in honor of Periyava. As the procession moved through the streets, Periyava looked around, searching for Ramanathan Chettiar, but he was nowhere to be seen. After the procession ended and Periyava returned to the Mutt, he stepped out of the palanquin and noticed Ramanathan Chettiar standing quietly to the side.

Periyava called him and asked, "Where were you during the procession? I was searching for you."

Overwhelmed by Periyava's concern, tears welled up in Ramanathan Chettiar's eyes as he humbly replied, "Periyava! I was with you throughout the procession. I was carrying your palanquin on my shoulder. I was blessed with the rare fortune of carrying you."

At that moment, he sang five pamalai (a garland of verses) in praise of Periyava. Deeply moved, Periyava asked him to recite and explain the meaning of the hymns to the assembled devotees.

Periyava's Concern for Language and Culture

While in Kariapatti, Sri Pandithamani M.U. Kathiresan Chettiar, a great scholar in Tamil and Sanskrit, came to meet Periyava. Their conversation turned to the growing influence of Western culture and the declining interest in Indian languages and traditions. Periyava expressed his concern:

> *"People are drifting away from our own rich literature, culture, and languages. The number of those who understand and uphold our traditions is dwindling rapidly. To preserve our heritage, we must uphold sacred languages like Sanskrit and Tamil."*

Turning to Kathiresan Chettiar, he said, "It is people like you who must come forward to safeguard our mother tongue, our culture, and our literature."

Kathiresan Chettiar, deeply moved by Periyava's faith in him, had tears in his eyes. "With Periyava's blessings, I will do everything I can to uphold our language and literature," he vowed. Before leaving, he made a humble request:

"Periyava, my only wish is that you always remember me."

Periyava smiled gently and said, "Of course, I will."

The Concerns of Annamalai Chettiar

Earlier, during his visit to Kanadukathan, Periyava had missed meeting Rajah Sir Annamalai Chettiar, who was away in Delhi at the time. Unable to bear the disappointment, Annamalai Chettiar earnestly requested Periyava to visit Kanadukathan again. Graciously accepting his request, Periyava returned to Kanadukathan, where he was received with an even grander reception and procession.

During their conversation, Annamalai Chettiar expressed his deep concern about the erosion of Sanatana Dharma and traditional values.

> *"Periyava, I wish that all mahans and Mathathipathis follow your example and undertake yatras across the country to uphold Sanatana Dharma and our sacred traditions."*

He lamented how the younger generation, particularly Brahmin children, were being drawn to Western culture. "These bright and intelligent children are getting educated in English and drifting away from their roots. The British are keen to attract them, and as they abandon our traditions, others follow. This pattern is causing our cultural values to fade away."

Periyava on Dowry and Social Issues

Annamalai Chettiar also raised concerns about the growing dowry system in the Brahmin community. "Due to high dowry demands, many girls remain unmarried, and this is causing great distress to families. This practice is against our culture and must be addressed. Periyava, please guide us on how to remove this evil from our society. Whatever you say, I will ensure it reaches the community and is implemented."

Periyava, pleased by Annamalai Chettiar's sincerity, reassured him: "I am glad you care so deeply for our culture and tradition. I will tell you the right course of action at the right time, and I will seek your support when needed."

Later, Periyava strongly opposed the dowry system, stating that it was against Shastras. He referenced Nigamananda Desika, a revered Vaishnava scholar, and narrated how, in his time, dowry was given by the groom to the bride, whereas in modern times, the practice had reversed, causing immense hardship.

To reinforce his stance, Periyava later instructed: "No one should use my name in wedding invitations if dowry is involved in the marriage."

Periyava's Views on Simplicity and Luxury

Periyava was also against the wearing of silk garments, as it created disparities between the rich and the poor. He believed that luxury created unnecessary desires among the less privileged, leading them to spend beyond their means just to keep up with societal expectations.

Similarly, Periyava discouraged coffee consumption, viewing it as an unnecessary indulgence. He remarked that while coffee was affordable for some, for many it was a luxury that distracted from essential needs. His concern was not just economic but also health-related, as he believed excessive coffee consumption could be harmful.

Through his own simple and austere life, Periyava set an example, embodying the true spirit of renunciation (sanyasa). Though emperors and kings fell at his feet, ready to offer him anything he wished for, he remained detached from material life, like a lotus leaf untouched by water.

A Muslim Devotee's Reverence

During his yatra from Karambakkudi to Pattukottai, after traveling about 5 kilometers, Periyava suddenly asked the procession to stop. Moments later, an elderly man came running behind them.

Periyava asked, "Who are you, and where have you come from?"

The old man replied, "I have come from Karambakkudi."

Periyava, puzzled, asked, "Then why didn't you meet me there?"

With folded hands, the man said, "I wanted to have darshan of Periyava in solitude (Ekantham)."

He then sang the verses he had composed in Periyava's praise. Periyava, touched by his devotion, asked him to sing them before the entire gathering.

At the end, the elderly man made a heartfelt request: "I always wish to think of Periyava. But more than that, I wish for Periyava to remember me forever."

To everyone's astonishment, the devotee was a pious Muslim elder. With tears in his eyes, he said, "Periyava, in our religion, we do not give a form to God. But if I were to envision Allah in a human form, I see Him as none other than Periyava."

This divine moment reaffirmed that Maha Periyava was truly Jagadguru – the Guru of the entire world, beyond barriers of religion, caste, or creed.

Bhakti and Destiny: The Pativrata's Prophecy and Periyava's Divine Journey

During his 21-year-long Kashi Yatra, Kanchi Maha Periyava placed great importance on *Bhakti* (devotion) and scholarship. As he traveled through Andhra Pradesh in the later years of his Yatra, he ensured that *Vidvath Sadas*—gatherings of scholars for scriptural debates—were conducted at every significant stop.

While in the Godavari district, a deeply moving incident unfolded, demonstrating Periyava's reverence for true devotion. A physically challenged man, unable to walk, was carried in a basket on his wife's head to seek Periyava's blessings. Witnessing this extraordinary act of love and dedication, Periyava was deeply moved. He praised the woman's *pativrata dharma*—the ideal of an unwaveringly devoted wife—and compared her to *Nalayani*, a legendary symbol of chastity and devotion.

Nalayani, Damayanti, epitomized devotion and selflessness. Married to Maharishi Maudgalya, she endured immense hardships with unwavering faith. Despite her husband's deliberate tests of her commitment, she remained steadfast in her service and love. Pleased by her dedication, Maudgalya ultimately revealed his true divine form and blessed her. Her virtue was so powerful that she was reborn as Draupadi in her next life, continuing to exemplify loyalty and endurance.

Periyava, recognizing the divinity in the woman's devotion, asked her, **"You are a great soul and a true pativrata. Tell me something about me—I wish to hear about myself from the mouth of a pativrata."**

With unwavering conviction, she replied, **"You are none other than Lord Eshwara himself. You will live for 100 years, less four Nakshatras."**

Decades later, her words proved to be prophetic. Maha Periyava attained *Siddhi* in January 1994. Had he lived until May 1994, he would have completed 100 years and stepped into his 101st year. However, as foretold, he departed precisely four *Anusha Nakshatrams* before his centenary.

Periyava's life itself became an affirmation of her divine blessing, proving that the words of a true *pativrata* hold the power of destiny.

Photo: Periyava picture taken in 1926 during his Yatra

15

MAHA PERIYAVA'S YATRA IN TRICHY & PUDUCHERRY (1926–1927)

In 1926, as Maha Periyava continued his divine yatra, he reached Thiruvanaikoil, a sacred town known for the revered Jambukeswarar Temple, one of the Pancha Bhoota Sthalams representing the water element. It was here that several distinguished personalities sought his darshan, including prominent political leaders and businessmen of that time.

Among those who arrived were Jamnalal Bajaj, a revered industrialist and close associate of Mahatma Gandhi, C. Rajagopalachari (Rajaji), a statesman who would later become India's first Governor-General, Dr. T.V. Swaminatha Sastri, a renowned scholar, and P. Jayarama Iyer, a respected administrator and devotee.

Periyava was staying on the first floor of the building where he was performing his daily rituals and upanyasams. While Jamnalal Bajaj, Dr. T.V. Swaminatha Sastri, and P. Jayarama Iyer went upstairs and had darshan of Periyava, Rajaji remained on the ground floor, deliberately avoiding the meeting.

Periyava, being an omniscient sage, was already aware of Rajaji's presence and immediately inquired about him. "Where is Rajaji?" he asked.

Jayarama Iyer respectfully replied, "Periyava, Rajaji is downstairs. He chose to stay back."

Periyava, with his characteristic compassion and insight, sensed something deeper in Rajaji's decision and instructed Jayarama Iyer, "Go and bring him here."

When Rajaji finally came upstairs, Periyava, with a serene smile, asked him, "Can I know why you did not come up on your own?"

With humility, Rajaji replied, "Periyava, I have not yet taken my bath, and hence, I did not want to have darshan in this state."

Periyava listened patiently and then responded with profound wisdom:

> "That's all? Rajaji, you are a man of Desha Sevai (national service). People like you, who have dedicated their entire lives to the country, do not have the luxury of personal time for rituals. You are clean from within—Ātmaśuddhi (purity of the soul) matters more than the external cleanliness of the body. There is no impurity in your actions or your service to the nation."

Rajaji was deeply moved by Periyava's words. His eyes welled up, and he bowed with gratitude, realizing the profound truth that inner purity and selflessness hold greater significance than mere external observances.

Periyava continued, providing an insightful example:

When one undertakes a Yagna Deeksha, they remain in a state of selflessness throughout the Yagna. They are not required to bathe until the Yagna is completed. The act of giving and self-sacrifice in a Yagna completes the spiritual cycle and ensures divine blessings. It reinforces the principles of dharma (righteousness) and daan (charity).

Likewise, Rajaji, you have taken the Deeksha for Bharata Desam's freedom. This same dharma applies to you as well. Do not let minor ritualistic concerns interfere with your noble mission.

Rajaji, a staunch follower of tradition and discipline, was overwhelmed by Periyava's words. He realized that his unwavering service to the country itself was a sacred Yagna, and Maha Periyava, the Jagadguru, had blessed him to continue with this divine responsibility.

Photo: Periyava picture taken in 1926 in his yatra at Udayarpalayam Lake

Periyava's Chaturmasya and Poojas in Kattumannarkoil and Thirupathiripuliyur

Following this episode, Periyava resumed his yatra and traveled to Kattumannarkoil, where he conducted the Chaturmasya Pooja and Vyasa Pooja with great devotion.

From there, he proceeded to Thirupathiripuliyur, an ancient town steeped in spiritual history. Here, Periyava performed the Navaratri Pooja at the Padaleeswarar Temple, one of the most sacred Shiva temples in Tamil Nadu.

This temple, believed to be over 2000 years old, holds a significant place in Shaivism. Lord Shiva is worshipped as Padaleeswarar, and Goddess Parvati as Periyanayaki. The temple's name is derived from the legend of Saint Vyagrapada (Pulikkal Munivar), who performed intense penance here and was blessed with the divine vision of Lord Shiva.

This temple is also one of the Thevara Paadal Petra Sthalams, celebrated in the sacred hymns of the Nayanmars—Appar, Sundarar, and Sambandar. The magnificent Raja Gopuram (tower) and intricate sculptures add to the temple's grandeur.

During Maha Periyava's stay, the town witnessed an influx of devotees, drawn by his divine presence.

Meeting with Achalambigai Ammaiyar: The Poetess of the Freedom Movement

During Periyava's time in Thirupathiripuliyur, a well-known Congress leader and ardent freedom fighter, Achalambigai Ammaiyar, came for his darshan. She was an active participant in the Gandhian movement and was known for writing Gandhi's life stories in Tamil.

However, her visit to Periyava was more personal.

Asalambigai Ammaiyar was once a student of Periyava's father, Sri Subramania Sastrigal. She had known Periyava as Swaminathan, a bright child with a divine aura. Now, standing before him as the Jagadguru, she was overwhelmed with emotion.

With tears in her eyes, she bowed before Periyava and sang five devotional songs that she had composed in his honor. The songs were filled with deep devotion and reverence, capturing the essence of his divine journey.

Periyava, with his characteristic humility, listened attentively, blessing her with his divine grace.

The Restoration of Thiruvarur's Chariot: Periyava's Divine Intervention

While in Thirupathiripuliyur, Yazhulur Subbarama Vathiyar approached Periyava with an important mission.

He was seeking Periyava's blessings and support for the renovation of the Thiruvarur temple's grand chariot (Ther). The temple chariot, which once stood as a magnificent symbol of devotion, had been destroyed by anti-social elements who set it on fire.

Subbarama Vathiyar, representing the people of Thiruvarur, expressed their deep desire to restore the chariot and revive the tradition of the Rathotsavam (chariot festival).

Periyava, recognizing the spiritual and cultural importance of the project, immediately donated ₹1000, a significant amount at the time, and provided a Srimugam (written blessing and authorization) for the cause.

Under Periyava's guidance, ₹1 lakh was collected within just six months for the chariot's restoration. Additionally, Periyava requested the Kerala devotees to contribute teakwood for the chariot's construction, ensuring the divine cause was fulfilled.

Subbarama Vathiyar, deeply touched by Periyava's blessings, later took Sannyasa and became known as Sri Narayana Brahmendrar, attaining Siddhi at Marudavancheri, chanting "Thyagesa, Thyagesa, Thyagesa," merging into the divine presence of Lord Thyagaraja Swamy.

16

MAHA PERIYAVA'S YATRA TO PUDUCHERRY AND BEYOND (1926–1927)

In 1926, Maha Periyava continued his divine yatra to Puducherry (formerly Pondicherry), marking a significant milestone in his journey. This was Periyava's first visit to Puducherry, following in the footsteps of the 66th Acharya of Kanchi Kamakoti Peetam, Sri Chandrasekarendra Saraswati Swamigal, who had visited the town in 1906.

The French government, which ruled Puducherry at the time, held the Acharyas of Kanchi Kamakoti Mutt in the highest regard. As a mark of deep respect, whenever the Peetadhipathi of Kanchi Mutt visited, the French administration organized a grand reception. The entire town would be decorated, and a royal welcome would be extended. Upon Periyava's arrival, cannons were ceremoniously fired as a salute, and the Governor, along with his family and senior officials, would personally receive Periyava with *Poorna Kumbham*. This honor reflected the reverence the French government had for the spiritual leadership of the Kanchi Acharyas.

After completing his yatra in Puducherry, Periyava proceeded to Vadavambalam, a small but historically significant village closely associated with Kanchi Mutt. It was in this village that the 58th Peetadhipathi, Sri Atma Bodhendra Saraswati Swamigal, had attained *Siddhi* nearly 300 years earlier.

Rediscovery of Sri Atma Bodhendra Saraswati Swamigal's Adhishtanam

Sri Atma Bodhendra Saraswati Swamigal, a great saint of the Kanchi Kamakoti Peetam, was a key proponent of *Nama Siddhanta*—the philosophy that the constant chanting of the Lord's name, especially *Rama Nama*, is the simplest and most effective path to Moksha in Kali Yuga, he was initiated into *Sannyasa* by his guru, Sri Paramasivendra Saraswati Swamigal. His final resting place (*Adhishtanam*) was originally on the banks of the Thenpennai River, but due to erosion over centuries, the precise location had been lost to time.

During his visit to Vadavambalam in 1927, Maha Periyava expressed a deep desire to locate the *Adhishtanam* of Sri Atma Bodhendra Saraswati Swamigal. He inquired among the local residents, but no one had any knowledge of its location, as it had been submerged and forgotten for three centuries.

Periyava, with his divine intuition, walked across the entire village, tirelessly searching for the sacred site. Eventually, he arrived at a banana plantation and stood still at a particular spot. He turned to those accompanying him and asked, "Could this be the place?" The villagers, however, dismissed the idea, stating that the land had been farmland for generations, making it highly unlikely.

Without hesitation, Periyava instructed a *Mutt* member, Kumaramangalam Sambamoorthy Sastrigal, to bring a *manvetti* (a traditional Indian digging tool). Periyava pointed to a specific spot and asked him to dig. Sambamoorthy Sastrigal obeyed and began digging. As the hours passed, more and more villagers gathered to witness the event.

After digging approximately 10 to 15 feet, the *manvetti* suddenly struck something hard. As he continued to explore the spot, he unearthed a skull. At that very moment, Sambamoorthy Sastrigal let out a loud cry, shouting, "Stop! Stop! Stop! Sadasivam! Sadasivam! Sadasivam!" before fainting inside the pit.

Maha Periyava calmly instructed everyone to mark the location and then returned to the *Mutt* and perform his daily *puja* rituals.

The Divine Vision of Sambamoorthy Sastrigal

Once he regained consciousness, Sambamoorthy Sastrigal narrated his extraordinary experience to Periyava and others. He described how, as he was digging, he had a divine vision—a small child appeared in the form of a *sannyasi*, and as he continued digging, the child grew larger and larger until it became a towering figure, extending from the sky to the earth in *Vishwaroopam*, still in the *sannyasi* form. The divine figure was chanting, *Sadasivam! Sadasivam! Sadasivam!* He also saw hundreds of *Vedic* scholars gathered before the saint, chanting sacred hymns. Overwhelmed by this divine revelation, he had instinctively shouted and collapsed.

This vision provided irrefutable proof that the skull belonged to Sri Atma Bodhendra Saraswati Swamigal.

Establishment of the Adhishtanam

Following this discovery, Periyava sought the assistance of Valavanoor Ramaswamy Iyer, a devoted follower of the Kanchi Mutt. He requested Ramaswamy Iyer to take the initiative in acquiring the land so that a proper *Adhishtanam* could be reestablished. With Periyava's blessings, the land was procured, and on January 17, 1927, the *Brindavanam* and *Adhishtanam* of Sri Atma Bodhendra Saraswati Swamigal were formally consecrated. Even today, devotees visit this sacred site and experience divine grace through the chanting of *Rama Nama*.

Periyava's Wisdom on Divine Destiny

At a later date, Ramaswamy Iyer suggested to Periyava that an arch should be erected at the entrance of Vadavambalam to publicize the location of the *Adhishtanam* so that more devotees could visit. Periyava, however, gently declined, saying:

"Now, Periyava is in solitude (Ekantam). Why should we disturb him? If a person has praptam (divine eligibility), he will automatically receive the blessings to visit this sacred place. Periyava will decide who should come."

This profound statement underscores the principle that divine experiences cannot be forced upon people—they occur only when the individual is truly ready and destined to receive them.

Continuing the Yatra – Cuddalore, Virudhachalam, and Beyond

From Vadavambalam, Periyava continued his yatra to Cuddalore and Virudhachalam. Virudhachalam holds special significance as the birthplace of Sri Atma Bodhendra Saraswati Swamigal.

The Virudhachalam Sri Vriddhagiriswarar Temple, also known as Pazhamalai Nathar Temple, is one of Tamil Nadu's oldest and most revered Shiva temples. Dedicated to Lord Vriddhagiriswarar, a *Swayambhu Lingam*, the temple is glorified in *Thevaram* hymns by the Nayanmars, making it a *Paadal Petra Sthalam*. It is believed that Lord Shiva himself performed miracles here, bestowing wisdom and longevity upon devotees. The temple hosts grand celebrations during *Maha Shivaratri* and *Arudra Darshan*, drawing thousands of devotees.

Periyava then traveled through Kallakurichi, Attur, and reached Salem.

An Islamic Scholar in Sanskrit

During his stay in Salem, Periyava was deeply impressed when an Islamic scholar presented a poem in Sanskrit. Astonished by the scholar's proficiency, Periyava inquired about his background. The scholar humbly explained that his ancestors, including his father and grandfather, had been well-versed in Sanskrit, which had inspired him to master the language. Periyava encouraged him to continue preserving and promoting Sanskrit, urging him to train future students in this divine knowledge.

Witnessing the Scenic Beauty of the Cauvery at Nerinjipettai

In Nerinjipettai, Periyava walked several miles across the hills to witness the spot where the Cauvery River enters Tamil Nadu. He was known to appreciate nature's beauty, and this visit was one of those moments where he admired the divine creation.

Arrival in Coimbatore and Palakkad

By April 1927, Periyava arrived in Coimbatore, where he stayed at the Sringeri Mutt, performing all the prescribed rituals with great reverence. Unlike today's scenario, where divisions exist between different *Mutts*, Periyava never showed any distinction, treating all *Mutts* with equal respect—an embodiment of his universal wisdom.

From Coimbatore, Periyava proceeded to Palakkad in Kerala, the birthplace of Adi Shankaracharya, thus continuing his extraordinary spiritual journey.

17

MAHA PERIYAVA'S YATRA TO KERALA (1927-1928)

After his visit to Coimbatore, Maha Periyava continued his yatra to Kerala, a land deeply intertwined with mythology, spirituality, and ancient traditions. Kerala is revered as "Parashurama Kshetram" because, according to Hindu scriptures, it was reclaimed from the sea by Sage Parashurama, the sixth avatar of Lord Vishnu. This divine act made Kerala a land of immense spiritual energy, home to numerous temples consecrated by Parashurama himself.

However, Kerala also carries an ancient curse: Kshatriyas (the warrior class) were forbidden from entering the land. This belief stemmed from the legend of Parashurama's battles against the Kshatriyas, after which he established Kerala as a land meant for Brahmins and ascetics.

The Legend of Kerala's Creation

Sage Parashurama was the son of Sage Jamadagni and Renuka. When his father was unjustly slain by King Kartavirya Arjuna, Parashurama took a vow to eliminate corrupt Kshatriya rulers. He waged 21 battles, eradicating oppressive kings and eventually donating all the conquered lands to Rishi Kasyapar.

Having renounced everything, he sought a place where righteous people could live in peace. He undertook severe penance to Lord Varuna (the ocean god) at Gokarna, pleading for land. Varuna granted his wish, and Parashurama hurled his divine axe (Parashu) into the sea. The waters miraculously receded, revealing a new stretch of land—Kerala, extending from Gokarna to Kanyakumari.

To ensure the sanctity of the land, Parashurama invited Brahmins to settle there, consecrating several temples. However, as per the divine decree, Kshatriyas were forbidden from setting foot in the land, lest they incur Brahmahatya Dosha (the sin of slaying Brahmins or holy sages).

Periyava's Pilgrimage through Kerala

Sacred Dip at Saraganga Theertham

During his journey, Maha Periyava performed the Chaturmasya Vratam in Kanchikodu in 1927. From there, he traveled to Parai, near the Tamil Nadu-Kerala border. At this location flows the Walayar River, which naturally demarcates the two states. Here, Maha Periyava took a holy dip in the Saraganga Theertham—a sacred water body with an extraordinary legend.

According to Hindu tradition, when Lord Rama and Lakshmana were en route to Lanka, they arrived at the banks of the Walayar River. Rama, unaware of the ancient curse, swam across and set foot on Parashurama's land. Lakshmana, recognizing the implications, cautioned him:

> *"This land is Parashurama's domain. As per his decree, no Kshatriya should enter. If they do, they will incur the terrible sin of Brahmahatya Dosha. To absolve oneself, one must take a dip in the holy Ganges."*

Rama, however, could not turn back to travel to the north for a Ganga Snanam, as his duty lay in Lanka. Realizing this, he invoked Ganga Devi with intense devotion. He then took his bow and struck a rock with an arrow. Miraculously, pure Ganga water began to gush forth from the split rock. This divine spring was named Saraganga, meaning 'Ganga born from an arrow.' To this day, Saraganga continues to flow, and devotees believe that bathing here absolves one of sins.

Maha Periyava, fully aware of its sacred significance, took a ritualistic dip in the Saraganga Theertham. In later years, he narrated the story of Saraganga to his devotees, emphasizing the deep spiritual connections between different holy sites across India.

Meeting with Mahatma Gandhi – A Historic Interaction

In October 1927, Maha Periyava proceeded to the 18 Agraharams of Palakkad before reaching Nellicherry. Here, he stayed in a humble gosala (cowshed) attached to a devotee's house. It was in this serene and spiritually charged setting that Mahatma Gandhi visited Periyava on October 15, 1927 to seek his blessings and wisdom.

C. Rajagopalachari (Rajaji) accompanied Gandhi to this meeting. While Gandhi spoke in Hindi, Periyava responded in Sanskrit, demonstrating his mastery over multiple languages and his deep-rooted adherence to tradition. The discussion between the two great souls lasted a long time, but Periyava later revealed only selective aspects of it.

Neelam Raju Venkataseshah, editor of *Andhra Prabha* and a devoted follower of Periyava, later inquired about this conversation. Periyava, true to his principles of dharma, refused to disclose sensitive details, stating:

"A conversation between two individuals should remain private if one of them is no longer alive. It is unjust to reveal details that cannot be verified. This is the path of Dharma."

Even so, Periyava shared a few key insights from his discussion with Gandhi:

1. **True Freedom Lies Beyond Political Liberation** Periyava urged Gandhi to remind the people that freedom from British rule should not be the ultimate goal. True liberation lies in Mukti (spiritual freedom). Without devotion to Dharma and Bhakti (faith in God), political independence alone would be meaningless. Inspired by Periyava's words, Gandhi began integrating devotional songs like "Raghupati Raghava Raja Ram" into his freedom movement, spreading Bhakti along with patriotism.

2. **The Hindu-Muslim Divide & the Need for Harmony** Gandhi expressed his deep sorrow over the brutal murder of Swami Shraddhananda, a Hindu monk who was assassinated by a radical. Gandhi lamented how British policies had created divisions between Hindus and Muslims, leading to tragic communal violence.

Periyava's reply was prophetic

"Gandhi, no community should be blamed for the actions of a few. There are noble and wicked individuals in every faith. If a Hindu were to kill you or me, should we hold the entire Hindu community accountable?"

Twenty years later, this very insight would become painfully relevant when Nathuram Godse, a Hindu, assassinated Gandhi. This demonstrated Periyava's ability as a Trikala Jnani (one who sees the past, present, and future).

Pilgrimage to Thrissur – The Land of Vadakkunnathan

In 1928, Maha Periyava visited Guruvayur and Thrissur, the latter known as Thiru-Shiva-Perur (The Land of Lord Shiva). He offered prayers at the Vadakkunnathan Temple, one of the oldest Shiva temples in India.

The Eternal Ghee Offering

A unique feature of Vadakkunnathan Temple is that the Shiva Lingam is entirely covered in layers of ghee, which never spoils. Devotees believe that consuming a small portion of this ghee has medicinal and spiritual benefits.

Additionally, this temple holds great significance for Adi Shankaracharya. His parents prayed here for a child, and Lord Shiva blessed them, saying he himself would be born as their son. Thus, Adi Shankaracharya was a divine incarnation of Lord Shiva.

Further Yatra & Royal Honours

Periyava continued his journey, receiving royal honors from the King of Kochi in Ernakulam. From there, he visited Vaikom, Trivandrum, and Alappuzha before returning to Tamil Nadu, stopping at Thiruvedagam, a temple linked to Thirugnana Sambandar's spiritual victory over Jain scholars.

In Solavandan, the Mysore Maharaja gifted an elephant to the Mutt, recognizing Periyava's divine stature. Later, in Ammainayakkanur, Ramaswamy Nayakar donated 300 acres of land to the Mutt, marking yet another milestone in Periyava's spiritual and administrative contributions.

This chapter beautifully showcases Maha Periyava's spiritual wisdom, his commitment to dharma, and his far-reaching impact on individuals, including Mahatma Gandhi. His journey through Kerala was not just a pilgrimage but a reaffirmation of Sanatana Dharma's eternal values.

Photo: Periyava picture taken in 1929

18

Maha Periyava's Yatra to Manaloor Pettai (1928–1929)

The Yatra Continues: Devotion, Suffering, and Divine Grace

After the Navaratri festival in Ammainayakkanur, Maha Periyava continued his yatra to Palani, one of the six sacred abodes (Arupadai Veedu) of Lord Murugan. The Palani Murugan Temple holds immense spiritual significance. It is believed that Lord Murugan, in his divine wisdom, chose Palani as his abode after realizing that true knowledge is the greatest wealth. The deity, Dhandayuthapani, is depicted as a youthful ascetic, symbolizing renunciation and self-realization. The idol, made of Navapashanam, a rare medicinal composition by Siddhar Bhogar, is believed to have immense spiritual and healing properties.

At the foothills of Palani stands Thiru Avinankudi, an ancient temple where Lord Murugan was worshipped as a child. This sacred place is considered older than the hill temple and signifies divine grace and the ultimate pursuit of knowledge. Periyava offered his prayers at Palani and then continued his journey to Thirukoilur.

Thirukoilur: The Land of Divine Grace and Devotion

Thirukoilur, a sacred town in Tamil Nadu, is renowned for the Ulagalantha Perumal Temple and the Veeratteswarar Temple. The Ulagalantha Perumal Temple is one of the 108 Divya Desams, where Lord Vishnu, in his Trivikrama (Vamana) avatar, subdued the demon king Mahabali, symbolizing divine grace over ego. The Veeratteswarar Temple, one of the eight Ashta Veeratta Sthalams, is where Lord Shiva performed acts of divine valor, specifically destroying the demon Andhakasura.

Thirukoilur is also deeply connected to the Vaishnava Alwars. It was here that Poigai, Bhoothath, and Pey Alwars met and composed the first hymns of the Naalayira Divya Prabandham, marking the beginning of Tamil devotional literature. This town, with its profound spiritual heritage, embodies divine intervention, victory over arrogance, and the devotional spirit of Tamil saints.

The Testing Times: Periyava's Malaria in Manaloor Pettai (1929)

In 1929, Maha Periyava reached Manaloor Pettai for the Vyasa Pooja. On 21st July 1929, he performed the pooja, offering his prayers with unwavering devotion. However, a few days later, on 24th July 1929, Periyava's Poorvashrama father, Sri Subramanya Sastrigal, passed away in Kumbakonam. Around the same time, Periyava was struck by a severe bout of malaria.

For over a month, Periyava suffered intense fever, weakness, and immense physical discomfort. Devotees and disciples repeatedly urged him to take medicines and undergo treatment. However, Periyava, deeply rooted in his spiritual discipline, refused. He consumed only Thulasi Theertham (holy basil water) and continued to endure the suffering with absolute surrender to divine will.

Despite the excruciating illness, Periyava never compromised on his daily rituals. With unwavering discipline, he took his sacred baths at the prescribed times, performed the Chandramauleshwara Pooja, and fulfilled his spiritual duties with utmost dedication. This period exemplified Periyava's transcendence beyond bodily consciousness.

Periyava: Beyond Bodily Consciousness (Śarīra Prajñā)

Maha Periyava is often revered as a divine being who transcended Śarīra Prajñā (bodily awareness). Unlike ordinary humans who rely on bodily instincts—hunger, thirst, and the need for rest—Periyava lived in a state beyond such physical limitations. His life embodied vairāgya (detachment) and tapas (austerity), demonstrating complete mastery over bodily needs.

The Yoga Vasishta records a moment when Lord Rama, overwhelmed by human emotions, was reminded by Sage Vasishta of his divine nature. Rama responded with the following profound sloka:

"Atmanam manye Ramaṁ, dvirahitam anyaṁ na manye"

(आत्मानं मन्ये रामं, द्विरहितं अन्यं न मन्ये)

Meaning:
"I consider myself as Atman (the Supreme Self); apart from that, I do not see any second entity."

This reflects the essence of Advaita philosophy, where the realized being exists beyond duality. Maha Periyava lived by this very realization—though engaged in worldly activities, he remained firmly established in non-duality. Even when devotees expressed concern for his health, he remained indifferent, subtly indicating that he had transcended bodily identification.

Photo: Periyava picture taken in 1929

Marathi Swamigal: The Devotee Who Became a Guardian

At this critical juncture, a divine intervention occurred. A great Mahan, Marathi Swamigal, arrived in March 1929. A Sannyasi from the north, he was on his way to Rameswaram for a sacred pilgrimage. For North Indians, Rameswaram holds the same spiritual significance as Kashi does for South Indians.

During his return journey from Rameswaram, Marathi Swamigal lost his Dhandam (ascetic's staff). As per Sannyasa Dharma, a monk cannot simply replace a lost Dhandam with any stick; it must be received through a prescribed ritual from another ascetic. Desperate to find a Guru in the South, he learned about Maha Periyava and traveled to Manaloor Pettai.

Upon meeting Periyava, he humbly requested him to grant a new Dhandam. Periyava, understanding the gravity of the request, performed the necessary rituals and handed him the sacred staff. From that moment on, Marathi Swamigal remained with Periyava for the next 25 years, eventually attaining Siddhi in Kanchipuram.

Despite his fiery temperament, Marathi Swamigal was a Maha Tapasvi—a great ascetic. He took on the role of Periyava's devoted caretaker. Every morning, he would bathe, gather fresh flowers, grind sandalwood paste, and perform Patha Pooja (worship of Periyava's feet). While doing so, tears of devotion flowed from his eyes.

Years later, Periyava recounted this incident in Bharatiya Vidya Bhavan's journal, in a series titled "What Life Has Taught Me?", written exclusively by spiritual luminaries.

Marathi Swamigal's Supreme Devotion: The Tirupati Incident (1932)

In 1932, while on his Kashi Yatra, Maha Periyava reached Tirupati. As a young ascetic, he climbed the hill swiftly. However, Marathi Swamigal, being older, struggled to match Periyava's pace. By the time he reached the temple entrance, Periyava had completed his darshan.

Realizing this, Periyava requested the temple authorities to allow Marathi Swamigal inside for a special darshan. However, Swamigal's response left everyone astonished.

"Why?" he asked.

The temple authorities were taken aback—why would a devotee decline darshan? Swamigal then pointed to Maha Periyava and said, "Balaji is already here before me."

This profound statement revealed Marathi Swamigal's realization that Periyava was none other than Lord's avatara. He did not need a separate darshan, as he was already in the divine presence of Periyava.

Surrender of a Devotee: The Farmer of Thandalam

After completing Chaturmasyam Pooja in Manaloor Pettai, Periyava visited Villupuram—his birthplace. The town that had once seen a young boy grow into a scholar now welcomed him as Jagadguru. From there, Periyava continued to Tindivanam and then to Thandalam.

In Thandalam, a simple farmer, overwhelmed with devotion, surrendered himself to Periyava. Seeing others offering donations, he believed it was necessary to give something. Since he had nothing to offer, he sold his land and placed the money at Periyava's feet.

Periyava, deeply moved yet concerned, inquired about the source. When he learned the truth, he refused to accept it. However, the farmer insisted, saying, "I offer this to Lord Shiva in your form."

This ultimate act of surrender—Saranagati—demonstrated the depth of his Bhakti.

These incidents illuminate the profound devotion, sacrifices, and divine experiences that surrounded Maha Periyava. Whether it was enduring extreme suffering, receiving unwavering devotion, or guiding sincere seekers, Periyava's life was a living testament to Sanatana Dharma's eternal wisdom.

ॐ

19

Maha Periyava's Yatra in Tiruvannamalai to Arcot (1929–1930)

Chapter: The Eternal Light of Arunachala – Maha Periyava's Visit to Tiruvannamalai

In the year 1929, during his Vijaya Yatra, *Jagadguru Sri Chandrasekarendra Saraswati Swamigal*, known as Maha Periyava, arrived at the sacred town of Tiruvannamalai to witness the grand Karthigai Deepam festival. This journey was not just another stop in his divine pilgrimage but a momentous event that reaffirmed the spiritual essence of Arunachala, the mountain revered as Lord Shiva Himself.

Tiruvannamalai – The Flame of Jnana

The Arunachaleswarar Temple in Tiruvannamalai is one of the holiest shrines of Lord Shiva, enshrining the Agni Lingam, representing the cosmic fire of creation and destruction. According to legend, Lord Shiva once manifested as an infinite column of fire to humble Lord Brahma and Lord Vishnu, who were debating their supremacy. Neither could find the beginning nor the end of Shiva's form, leading to the establishment of the sacred *Karthigai Deepam* festival. Each year, an enormous beacon is lit atop Arunachala Hill, symbolizing Shiva's boundless light and presence.

Tiruvannamalai is also a profound center for seekers on the path of *Jnana* (self-realization). Saints such as Seshadri Swamigal, Bhagavan Ramana Maharshi meditated in its serene landscape, recognizing Arunachala as the embodiment of the Supreme Truth. The 14-kilometer circumambulation of the hill, known as Girivalam, is believed to absolve sins and bestow liberation (*moksha*). The entire mountain is revered as a Lingam, and in Sanatana Dharma, it is said that just by remembering Arunachala (*Smaranath Arunachalam*), one can attain salvation.

Moksha Through Four Sacred Paths

Sanatana Dharma describes four unique ways to attain Moksha:

1. **Birth in Thiruvarur** – A soul born in this sacred town is believed to attain liberation without a next birth.
2. **Death in Kashi (Varanasi)** – A person who breathes their last in Kashi is granted direct salvation.
3. **Darshan of Chidambaram Nataraja** – Those who witness the divine dance of Lord Shiva at Chidambaram achieve *Moksha*.
4. **Remembrance of Arunachala** – Merely thinking of Arunachala with devotion ensures liberation.

Periyava, being the very embodiment of wisdom, recognized the unparalleled spiritual significance of Tiruvannamalai and undertook the *Girivalam*, immersing himself in the divine energy of Arunachala.

Bringi Rishi and the Lesson of Ardhanarishvara

During his stay, Periyava spoke about Bringi Rishi, an ardent devotee of Lord Shiva. Bringi Rishi worshipped only Shiva, ignoring Devi Parvati, the universal mother. To teach him a lesson, Goddess Parvati merged completely with Lord Shiva, making it impossible for Bringi to separate them. Undeterred, Bringi transformed into a beetle and tried to bore through their divine form to worship only Shiva. Recognizing his unwavering devotion, Lord Shiva granted him a third leg to stand independently, as Parvati had withdrawn her energy from him.

This incident, which took place in Tiruvannamalai, conveys a profound message—Shiva and Shakti are inseparable. One cannot exist without the other, just as creation and dissolution are intertwined in the cosmic balance.

The Infinite Light – The Legend of Arunachala Jyoti

One of the most sacred events in Tiruvannamalai is the Lingodbhava manifestation of Lord Shiva. To humble Lord Brahma and Lord Vishnu, Shiva took the form of an endless column of fire. Brahma, in the form of a swan, ascended the skies to find the top, while Vishnu, as a boar, burrowed deep to reach the bottom. Unable to succeed, Vishnu humbly accepted his defeat, but Brahma falsely claimed victory by producing a *Ketaki flower* as proof. Enraged by the deception, Shiva cursed Brahma, stating that he would never have temples dedicated to him.

This *Jyotirlinga* manifestation at Tiruvannamalai is commemorated annually through the Siva Rathri, symbolizing the eternal and boundless nature of Shiva.

Maha Periyava and the Upholding of Dharma

During his stay in Tiruvannamalai, an incident occurred that highlighted Periyava's steadfast adherence to Sannyasa Dharma. One afternoon, while Periyava was engrossed in reading, a woman entered his room in distress. She directly approached him, sobbed, confessed something, and left. This was unusual, as no ladies was allowed into Periyava's presence without permission.

After she left, Periyava called the *Mutt* manager and asked, "How am I?" The manager, confused, hesitated. Periyava repeated the question, prompting the manager to reply, "Periyava is Jothi Swaroopam, Thejo Mayam!"

Periyava then asked, "What is my age?" The manager replied, "Around 45, Periyava."

Then, he asked, "What is my ashrama?" The manager answered, "Sannyasa Ashram, Periyava."

Periyava then solemnly stated, "A Sannyasi must uphold Brahmacharya (celibacy) in thought, word, and deed. Allowing a lone woman to enter my room is unacceptable. Even if I am as pure as fire, others must not be given the opportunity to question my conduct."

Realizing his mistake, the manager was devastated. Periyava firmly instructed, "From now on, no woman should meet me alone. They must always be accompanied by some male."

This incident underscores the extraordinary discipline with which Periyava upheld Dharma, ensuring that even the slightest scope for misinterpretation was avoided.

After witnessing the divine spectacle of Karthikai Deepam, Periyava continued his Vijaya Yatra, traveling through Sengam, Arur, and Dharmapuri, eventually reaching Hogenakkal.

Hogenakkal – The Niagara of India

Hogenakkal, often called the "Niagara of India," is a breathtaking waterfall on the sacred Kaveri River, located at the border of Tamil Nadu and Karnataka. The name Hogenakkal means "Smoking Rocks" in Kannada, referring to the mist created as the mighty river crashes onto jagged rocks, producing a mesmerizing view. The waters here are believed to have medicinal properties, as they flow through dense forests rich in herbal plants. This makes Hogenakkal a well-known destination for therapeutic baths and traditional oil massages.

The Kaveri River is deeply revered in Hindu tradition, and many pilgrims visit Hogenakkal to bathe in its waters, believing that doing so will cleanse them of sins. Additionally, the unique coracle boat rides on the swirling waters provide an unforgettable experience. This region is not only a natural marvel but also a place of spiritual and cultural significance.

Periyava, who always found solace in nature's lap, spent time in deep Dhyanam (meditation) here before continuing his journey.

Mekedatu – The Goat's Leap

From Hogenakkal, Periyava proceeded to Megathathu, better known as Mekedatu, which means "Goat's Leap" in Kannada. Located around 90 kilometers from Bengaluru, Mekedatu is a stunning spot where the Kaveri River, which is over 150 meters wide upstream, suddenly narrows into a rocky gorge just 10 meters wide.

According to legend, a goat once leaped across this narrow gorge while being chased by a tiger, and the tiger, unable to make the jump, was forced to retreat—hence the name Mekedatu. The location is part of the Cauvery Wildlife Sanctuary, which serves as a crucial link between the Biligiri Ranga Hills and Male Mahadeshwara Hills Tiger Reserves, making it vital for biodiversity conservation.

Periyava spent time in this sacred land before continuing his yatra.

A Miraculous Incident in Poosiamalaikuppam

In 1930, Periyava reached Poosimalaikuppam, a dense forest area, where he performed Vyasa Puja and observed the Chaturmasya

Vrata. Deep in the tranquil forest, Periyava engaged in severe penance (Tapas), enjoying the peace and solitude that nature provided.

The Elephant's Devotion

During his stay in the forest, a remarkable event occurred. One day, the elephant shed caught fire, causing the elephants to panic. One of the elephants, terrified and suffering from burns, fled deep into the forest and took refuge in a pond.

The elephant's mahout (caretaker) and others searched tirelessly and eventually found the elephant lying in the water, refusing to come out despite repeated coaxing. No one could understand why the elephant refused to move. Clueless, they approached Periyava for guidance.

Periyava, with his divine wisdom, simply smiled and walked to the pond. The moment the elephant saw Periyava, it immediately stood up, walked out of the water, and approached him. It then began making sounds, as if trying to communicate something. Though others could not understand, Periyava, being a Sarvagnan (omniscient one), understood the elephant's pain.

Periyava instructed the Mutt Manager to summon a veterinarian. Upon examination, it was found that the elephant had suffered burns on one side of its body. Thanks to Periyava's intervention, the elephant received treatment and was safely brought back to the camp.

This incident is reminiscent of the Gajendra Moksha episode in Hindu scriptures, where Lord Vishnu personally comes to the aid of an elephant in distress.

A Similar Incident: The Serpent in the Gosala

A similar divine event occurred sometime earlier in Kumbakonam. One night, a six-foot-long snake (Raja Nagam) slithered into the

Gosala (cowshed) where the cows and elephants were tied. The elephant began trumpeting loudly, and the cows started making distressed noises, alarming the Mutt members. When they checked, they found the enormous snake coiled inside.

Periyava arrived at the scene and instructed that no harm should come to the snake. Instead, he advised them to light a lamp and make a gentle noise to guide the snake out. The snake eventually left, but the elephant and cows remained restless and afraid.

Periyava, with his deep understanding of all living beings, remarked: *"Though the snake has left, the fear of the snake remains in their minds. Move them to another place, and they will find peace."*

Once the animals were moved, they calmed down immediately. This incident once again highlighted Periyava's profound connection with all creatures.

The Loyal Dog That Walked with Periyava

During Periyava's Vijaya Yatra in 1921, a stray dog began following the procession. The dog always walked alongside the palanquin, but never too close.

Periyava noticed this and frequently inquired: *"Has the dog been fed?"*

A particularly astonishing aspect of this dog's devotion was its Ekadashi fasting. On Ekadashi, Periyava would observe Nirjala Upavasam (fasting without even water), and on those days, the dog too would refuse to eat. Who taught the dog this devotion?

One day, some devotees threw stones at the dog. The dog retaliated, scaring them. Mistaking it for madness, the Mutt members blindfolded the dog, took it 8 km away, and released it. But by the time they returned to camp, the dog was already there, waiting for them.

When Periyava heard of this, he rebuked them, saying: *"You should not have done this. Someone threw a stone at the dog, and it reacted. It is not the dog's fault."*

After this, the dog became a beloved figure among Mutt members and devotees. People would ask, "Where is that dog?", and visiting devotees made sure to see it.

The Music Scholar and Periyava's Message on Harmony

During Periyava's Chaturmasyam in Poosimalaikuppam, several Vidwans (scholars) came for darshan. Among them was a Sri Vaishnava Vidwan, who started singing in front of Periyava.

Periyava, listening intently, asked: *"Do you know the meaning of this song?"*

The song was composed by a **Shaiva Bhakta** and contained a line that stated: *"As I am a Shiva Bhakta, I will not even look at a Vaishnava."*

Since the song was being sung by a **Vaishnava scholar**, Periyava wanted to highlight something profound. The singer **smiled and explained the meaning**.

Periyava then remarked: *"See, music has the power to **break barriers and unite people**. True devotion transcends all differences."*

After completing the Chaturmasyam pooja, Periyava resumed his yatra and arrived at Adaiyapalam, a small village in Tamil Nadu renowned as the birthplace of the great scholar and saint, Appaya Dikshitar (1520–1593). A distinguished Advaita Vedantin and prolific writer, Appaya Dikshitar authored over 100 works spanning Vedanta, Mimamsa, and Shaiva philosophy. He was a staunch proponent of Shaiva Advaita and played a crucial role in revitalizing Shaivism during his time. His unwavering devotion to Lord Shiva is evident in his celebrated compositions, including the *Margabandhu Stotram* and *Atmarpana Stuti*. Highly respected by kings and scholars alike, his influence extended far beyond his era. His life in Adaiyapalam was marked by intense spiritual practices, profound scholarly debates, and divine grace, making the village a site of immense historical and spiritual significance in Hindu philosophy.

From Adaiyapalam, Periyava continued his yatra to Virinchipuram, a sacred town near Vellore, famed for the ancient Margabandeswarar Temple dedicated to Lord Shiva. The temple derives its name from Lord Brahma (*Virinchi*), who is believed to have worshipped here. The presiding deity, Margabandeswarar, is revered as the divine guide and protector of travelers, ensuring their safe journey. The temple is also known for the sacred *Vajra Thoon* (Indestructible Pillar) and its unique Shiva Linga, which exudes divine energy.

Muthuswami Dikshitar, one of the Trinity of Carnatic music, composed the renowned kriti *Margabandho Mam Pahi* in praise of Lord Margabandeswarar. This composition beautifully extols Shiva as the ultimate protector of travelers and devotees, immortalizing the temple's significance in the world of Carnatic music and spirituality. Virinchipuram remains an important pilgrimage center, drawing both Shaivites and classical music enthusiasts.

From Virinchipuram, Periyava continued his yatra, visiting Kaveripakkam, Valaja Pettai, and finally reaching Arcot.

Arcot, historically known as *Shadaranyam* (the Land of Six Forests), holds immense spiritual and historical significance. The name *Shadaranyam* is believed to have originated from the six sacred forests that once surrounded the region, making it a center of deep spiritual energy and Vedic learning. Arcot is home to several ancient temples, including the renowned Jalakandeswarar Temple in Vellore, dedicated to Lord Shiva, and the Ranganatha Perumal Temple, dedicated to Lord Vishnu. The region has long been a confluence of Shaivism and Vaishnavism, attracting sages and saints who sought its serene environment for penance and meditation.

In addition to its spiritual prominence, Arcot played a pivotal role in South Indian history, serving as a strategic capital during the reign of the Nawabs and witnessing key battles between the British and the French. This unique blend of spiritual heritage and historical significance makes Arcot a place of great reverence and historical value.

The name *Shadaranyam* is also associated with six great rishis (sages) who are believed to have performed intense penance in this sacred region:

1. **Gautama Rishi** – Known for his deep meditation and the establishment of sacred rivers through his penance.
2. **Bharadwaja Rishi** – A great scholar and Vedic sage who contributed significantly to ancient Hindu scriptures.
3. **Agastya Rishi** – Revered for spreading Vedic knowledge and balancing the northern and southern energies of India.
4. **Kashyapa Rishi** – One of the Saptarishis, associated with the creation of various celestial beings and species.
5. **Atri Rishi** – A powerful sage, husband of Anasuya, known for his contributions to Vedic wisdom.
6. **Vasishta Rishi** – One of the foremost sages and preceptor to Lord Rama, renowned for his profound spiritual teachings.

These six rishis are believed to have chosen Arcot for their intense penance due to the region's sacred and spiritually energized atmosphere. The divine aura of their meditations is said to have sanctified the land, cementing Arcot's reputation as a place of great spiritual power.

Periyava also arrived in Arcot and stayed there, engaging in deep meditation and *tapas*, further enhancing the town's spiritual legacy.

20

Maha Periyava's Yatra and Paul Bruntan's Experience 1930

Periyava's Yatra: From Tiruvallur to Tiruvannamalai

After completing his Yatra in Arcot, Maha Periyava proceeded to Tiruvallur, a place of immense spiritual significance. The town is renowned for the Veera Raghava Perumal Temple, one of the 108 Divya Desams dedicated to Lord Vishnu. The presiding deity, Veera Raghava Perumal, is enshrined in a reclining posture (Bhujanga Sayanam), bestowing his divine blessings upon devotees, particularly for health and well-being. The temple is deeply associated with sage Salihotra, who performed intense penance at this sacred site, leading to the manifestation of Lord Vishnu to bless him. The temple's Hruthapa Nasini Theertham, the sacred tank, is believed to have divine healing powers, curing ailments and washing away sins.

Maha Periyava had a divine darshan at the temple and then continued his journey. It was during this time that Annadhana Sivan, a devout disciple of Periyava, attained Siddhi (spiritual liberation). Before his passing, he had left Rs. 160 with a friend in Trichy. This money was later given to Periyava, who decided that the first expenditure from this amount should be for a noble cause. Periyava instructed that the money be used for the renovation of a water tank in a Harijan colony, ensuring that the punniyam (spiritual merit) from this act of charity would go to Annadhana Sivan.

Thirumazhisai – The Land of Thirumazhisai Alvar

After Tiruvallur, Periyava reached Thirumazhisai, a highly revered town in Tamil Nadu, known as the birthplace of Thirumazhisai Alvar, one of the twelve Alvars who composed sacred hymns in praise of Lord Vishnu. This town is home to the Jagannatha Perumal Temple, a significant Divya Desam, where Lord Vishnu is worshipped in a rare seated posture, alongside Thirumangaivalli Thayar.

Another notable temple here is the Oordhvathandavam Murthi Temple, dedicated to Sri Yoga Narasimha, where it is believed that Lord Narasimha appeared before Thirumazhisai Alvar and his disciple Kanikkannan to restore righteousness. Thirumazhisai remains a place where devotion and divine grace are strongly manifest, attracting devotees seeking both material prosperity and spiritual upliftment.

Poonamallee – The Land of Thirukachi Nambi

From Thirumazhisai, Periyava continued his Yatra to Poonamallee, a town with both Vaishnavite and Saivite significance. Historically known as Pushpakamalli, named after a sacred jasmine flower, the town is closely associated with Thirukachi Nambi, the great devotee of Lord Vishnu and the guru of Sri Ramanujacharya.

The Vaidya Veeraraghava Perumal Temple, another Divya Desam, is a major pilgrimage center where Lord Vishnu is worshipped as Veeraraghava Perumal, a deity believed to grant relief from diseases. The town also houses the Sri Kasi Viswanathar Temple, where Lord Shiva and Goddess Vishalakshi bestow their divine blessings.

Additionally, Poonamallee is the birthplace of Thirukachi Nambi, who had divine conversations with Lord Varadaraja of Kanchipuram, making this town an important spiritual hub for both Vaishnavites and Saivites.

Koyambedu – A Sacred Village Turned Urban Hub

Periyava then reached Koyambedu, which, though today a bustling area in Chennai, was once a small spiritual village known as Kushalavapuri. According to legend, Lava and Kusha, the sons of Lord Rama, spent time here under the guidance of Sage Valmiki.

The place is particularly revered for the Kurungaleeswarar Temple, where Lord Shiva is worshipped as Kurungaleeswarar, and Goddess Parvati as Kampalavalli Thayar. It is believed that Goddess Parvati performed penance here in a dwarfed (kurun) form to reunite with Lord Shiva, which gave the deity his name. This temple, with its strong connections to the Ramayana and Saivism, adds to the sacred significance of Koyambedu.

Tirukazhukundram – The Hill of Divine Eagles

Periyava's Yatra continued to Tirukazhukundram, also known as Pakshi Theertham, famous for the Vedagiriswarar Temple, dedicated to Lord Shiva. The town derives its name from the Tamil words Kazhugu (eagle) and Kundram (hill), as it was believed that two sacred eagles visited the temple daily to receive offerings from the priests, a divine phenomenon that lasted for centuries until recent times.

The Sangu Theertham, a sacred temple tank, is believed to have a hidden conch (Sangu) that surfaces every 12 years, reinforcing the temple's sanctity. Maha Periyava performed Girivalam (circumambulation) of the hill, continuously chanting: "Deva, Deva Maha Deva, Vedha Vedha Maha Vedha…"

This sacred site is revered for its association with saints and sages who attained moksha through penance here.

Periyava and Paul Brunton – A Meeting of Spiritual Inquiry

As Periyava reached Chengalpattu, an interesting encounter took place. Paul Brunton, a British spiritual seeker and journalist, had been traveling through India, researching Sanatana Dharma and Indian philosophy. His journey led him to K.S. Venkata Ramani, a scholar, who informed him about Maha Periyava.

Upon meeting Periyava, Brunton was captivated by his divine presence, radiant face, and piercing eyes. He posed a profound question:

"What is the future of the world? Will people ever stop being violent and aggressive?"

Periyava, with his unparalleled wisdom, responded:

"The world has become overly materialistic. Nations today spend more on their military than on the well-being of their people. They invest heavily in destructive technologies, yet expect peace in return. How is that possible?"

Brunton then asked, "So, should we destroy all weapons to achieve peace?"

Periyava smiled and said:

"Do you think wars happen because weapons exist? No. People do not fight because they have weapons; they create weapons because they have a fighting tendency. Even if all weapons were destroyed, people would still fight with whatever they have in their hands. The root cause is the mind. The only way to eliminate conflict is through spiritual awakening. Only when the heart is filled with devotion and understanding can true peace prevail."

Brunton, deeply moved, inquired about Yogabhyāsam (spiritual discipline and yoga practice). Periyava replied:

"As a Mathadhipathi (head of a religious institution), I do not teach Yoga to individuals. However, I can direct you to two great masters. One resides in the forests and may or may not accept you. The other is in Tiruvannamalai—none other than Sri Ramana Maharishi."

Brunton heeded Periyava's advice and went to Tiruvannamalai, where he became a disciple of Ramana Maharishi.

That night, while resting in his room, Brunton experienced a miraculous vision. A sudden flash of light appeared in one corner of his dark room, and within that light, he saw the glowing face of Maha Periyava. The divine vision spoke:

"Maintain modesty. You will receive everything in life."

The vision disappeared, leaving Brunton in awe and deep spiritual realization. Later, he confirmed that this was not a dream, but a real divine experience.

These remarkable incidents highlight the profound wisdom, spiritual depth, and miraculous presence of Maha Periyava. His teachings on peace, spirituality, and discipline remain ever-relevant in today's turbulent world. Through these sacred travels and divine interactions, Periyava continued his mission—guiding seekers, uplifting dharma, and blessing the world with his divine wisdom.

21

Maha Periyava's Yatra to Kanchipuram and Chennai (1931–1932)

The Kashi Yatra and Maha Periyava's Visit to Kanchipuram, Kalahasti, and Tirupati (1931–1932)

Maha Periyava's Kashi Yatra was not just a pilgrimage but a divine mission to visit sacred sites. During this journey, He visited numerous sacred *tīrthas* (holy waters), temples, and spiritual centers, re-establishing their prominence and guiding devotees on the true essence of dharma.

Periyava's First Visit to Kanchipuram – The City of Moksha (25th January 1931)

On January 25, 1931, Maha Periyava visited Kanchipuram for the first time. Kanchipuram, one of the seven *Moksha-puris* (sacred cities that grant liberation), has been a beacon of spirituality, knowledge, and devotion for centuries. It is often referred to as the *City of Temples*, holding an unparalleled position in Hindu tradition due to its deep-rooted connections with Vedic scholarship and divine grace.

One of the most significant aspects of Kanchipuram is its association with Jagadguru Adi Shankaracharya, the great philosopher-saint who revived and firmly re-established Sanatana Dharma. According to *Shankara Vijayam*, Adi Shankaracharya installed the Sarvagna Peetam (Throne of Omniscience) in Kanchipuram, symbolizing his supreme mastery over scriptural knowledge. This *Peetam* was a declaration of Advaita Vedanta's authority, establishing Kanchipuram as an unparalleled center for spiritual wisdom, just as Kashmir and Kashi were known for their scholarly traditions.

Kanchipuram's spiritual prominence is also deeply intertwined with Goddess Kamakshi and the Kanchi Kamakoti Peetam. It is believed that Adi Shankaracharya attained Siddhi (Mahasamadhi) in Kanchipuram, reinforcing the city's divine status. His contributions to the Kamakshi Amman Temple are unparalleled, particularly the Yantra Pratishta (consecration of the Sri Chakra).

Historically, the Kamakshi Temple was a center of intense Shakti worship, where the Goddess was propitiated in her Ugra Swaroopa (fierce form) through rigorous tantric rituals. Adi Shankaracharya, recognizing the immense spiritual power in these practices, sought to harmonize the energies. To ensure that the Goddess's blessings were accessible to all devotees in a benevolent form, he consecrated the Sri Chakra Yantra beneath the main deity. This Bindu Peetam serves as a cosmic stabilizer, transforming the temple into a center for Sri Vidya Upasana, where Goddess Kamakshi is worshipped as Lalita Maha Tripurasundari, embodying supreme wisdom, grace, and compassion.

Through this divine act, Adi Shankara aligned Shakta traditions with Advaita Vedanta, blending bhakti (devotion) with jnana (wisdom). Even today, devotees believe that the Sri Chakra installed by him radiates immense spiritual energy, guiding seekers toward self-realization.

Photo: Periyava picture taken in 1931 in Kanchipuram

Photo: Periyava picture taken in 1931 Kanchipuram

22

Maha Periyava's Visit to Sri Kalahasteeswara Temple (1931–Maha Shivaratri)

From Kanchipuram, Maha Periyava continued His yatra and reached Sri Kalahasti in Andhra Pradesh to observe Maha Shivaratri in 1931.

Sri Kalahasti is renowned for the Sri Kalahasteeswara Temple, one of the Pancha Bhoota Sthalams, representing Vayu (Air) Tatva. The temple holds unique significance as the Dakshina Kailasam (Southern Kailash) and is revered for its Swayambhu Lingam, believed to radiate its own divine energy. Unlike traditional Lingams, abhishekam (ritual bathing) is not performed directly on the deity, as it is believed to naturally absorb all offerings.

The temple's very name—Kalahasti—derives from a profound legend of three devoted creatures:

- Kala (spider) – who wove intricate webs as offerings to Lord Shiva,
- Hasti (elephant) – who cleansed the Lingam daily with sacred waters,
- Sthi (serpent) – who adorned the deity with its hood as a divine offering.

Their intense devotion earned them divine liberation, making this temple a sacred pilgrimage site. Additionally, Sri Kalahasti is a prominent center for Rahu-Ketu Dosha Nivaran Pujas, attracting thousands seeking relief from planetary afflictions.

Maha Periyava had darshan at the temple and expressed His wish to circumambulate the Kalahasti hill (Girivalam). The hill has significance, Kannapa Nayanar worshiped the Lord on the top of the hill. Those accompanying Him hesitated due to the scorching sun and the rocky terrain, but Periyava walked effortlessly, unaffected by the heat, moving with divine grace through the rugged paths.

Later, the King of Kalahasti invited Periyava to his palace and performed Pada Puja (sacred feet worship) in devotion.

Maha Periyava's Arrival in Tirupati – Darshan of Lord Balaji

From Kalahasti, Periyava proceeded to Tirupati, where He had darshan of Lord Venkateshwara (Balaji) and Alarmel Mangai Thayar. His arrival in Tirupati was marked by grand celebrations, as devotees eagerly gathered to witness the Jagadguru's divine presence.

It is a well-known tradition that Kanchi Kamakoti Peetam Acharyas have special rights and privileges at Tirumala Temple, dating back to Adi Shankaracharya's time. Maha Periyava, as the *Peetadhipathi*, entered the Garbha Griha (sanctum sanctorum) and personally performed the Chamara Seva (fanning service) to Lord Balaji.

According to temple customs, if the Acharya's visit coincides with a Friday (Sukra Varam), he is granted the special honor of performing Abhishekam to Lord Balaji.

After completing His darshan, Periyava bathed in various holy *tīrthams* before proceeding to Venkatagiri, where He was warmly welcomed by the Venkatagiri Raja, who performed Pada Puja at his palace.

A Moment of Sanyasi Dharma – Periyava's Response to His Mother's Siddhi (14th June 1932)

As Periyava continued His yatra, He reached Nagari on June 14, 1932. During this time, a telegram arrived at the Mutt, and the manager rushed to deliver it while Periyava was presiding over a Sadas (spiritual assembly of scholars).

Before receiving the message, Periyava calmly asked the assembled scholars:

"If a Sanyasi's mother passes away, what should he do?"

The scholars were speechless, sensing the gravity of the moment. They soon realized that the telegram carried news of Maha Periyava's mother, Mahalakshmi Amma, attaining Siddhi in Kumbakonam.

There was a deep silence. The very woman who had given birth to the Jagadguru had now merged with the divine.

Without any visible emotion, Periyava took His *Danda* (staff) and walked towards the nearby Kailasa waterfalls. He remained there for a long time, immersing Himself in the sacred waters, observing silence (mouna) in the face of personal loss.

This incident left a profound impact on all present. It was a living demonstration of Vairagya (detachment)—the true path of a Sanyasi.

23

MAHA PERIYAVA'S FIRST VISIT TO CHENNAI (22ND SEPTEMBER 1932)

On September 22, 1932, the sacred feet of Maha Periyava touched the city of Chennai for the first time. Upon his arrival, he stayed at the Sanskrit College and performed the Navaratri Pooja with great devotion. During his stay, Periyava visited several prominent places in Chennai and delivered Upanyasams (spiritual discourses) every evening, drawing large gatherings of devotees who eagerly listened to his profound wisdom.

A significant moment from this visit was captured in a historic photograph taken in 1932 at the Sanskrit College, where Periyava is seen seated on a Silver Throne. This very place inside the college is preserved even today, and devotees can still witness the photograph, a timeless testament to his divine presence in the city.

In the later years, during 1957 and 1958, Periyava once again blessed Chennai with his presence and delivered a series of Upanyasams. These discourses, rich in spiritual wisdom and guidance, were later compiled and released as "Deivathin Kural" (The Voice of God) by Ra. Ganapathi, a revered devotee and chronicler of Periyava's teachings.

Photo: Periyava picture taken in 1932 Sanskrit College Chennai

Photo: Periyava picture taken in 1932 Sanskrit College Chennai

Photo: Periyava picture taken in 1932 Sanskrit College Chennai

Photo: Periyava picture taken in 1932 Sanskrit College Chennai

Devotees' Offerings and Yatra

One of Periyava's ardent devotees, Sri Dhandapani, the owner of PT Pani & Co., expressed his deep reverence by offering a Mena (Palanquin) for Periyava's yatra. This symbolic gesture reflected the unwavering devotion of his followers, who considered it their honor to facilitate Periyava's travels during his spiritual journey.

Visit to Thirumangalam

During his travels, Periyava was invited by Sri Ranganatha Iyer, a respected tile factory owner, to visit Thirumangalam. Accepting the request, Periyava stayed in Thirumangalam for several days, coinciding with the Pongal festival. His presence turned the town into a sacred hub, drawing people from far and wide to receive his blessings and listen to his divine words.

Meeting with MC Raja – A Testament to Atma Bhakti

A significant and much-discussed event during Periyava's journey was his meeting with MC Raja, a well-known leader from the Harijan (Scheduled Caste) community, who had even addressed the British Parliament in London.

Initially, there were concerns among the Mutts disciples and others, as they feared that MC Raja would demand temple entry rights, a topic that was under heated debate at the time. Since Periyava always upheld the Sastras and traditions, the Mutt members were apprehensive about a possible disagreement.

However, the meeting unfolded in a manner no one had expected. As soon as MC Raja saw Maha Periyava, he was deeply moved. The divine presence of Periyava overwhelmed him, and instead of initiating any debate, he surrendered himself with pure devotion (Atma Bhakti). Periyava, in his characteristic grace, advised MC Raja with compassion and wisdom, giving him spiritual guidance instead of engaging in any argument.

Such was the impact of this divine encounter that MC Raja's wife, overcome with reverence, took the very soil on which Periyava had walked and performed pooja in her home. This event left everyone astonished, as what was feared to be a potential confrontation ended in a profound display of humility and devotion.

This incident further reaffirmed the truth that Periyava's presence transcended societal and political barriers, and his interactions were always rooted in spiritual upliftment rather than worldly conflicts.

ॐ

24

MAHA PERIYAVA'S YATRA TO CHIDAMBARAM (1933–1934)

Periyava's Visit to Chidambaram: Breaking a 200-Year Barrier with Divine Grace

The Historical Context

In the year 1933, Kanchi Maha Periyava, Shri Chandrasekarendra Saraswathi Swamigal, visited the sacred town of Chidambaram, home to the illustrious Nataraja Swamy Temple, a place of unparalleled spiritual, architectural, and philosophical significance. This visit was not just another pilgrimage—it was a moment of great historical importance, as it marked the first time in 200 years that an Acharya of the Kanchi Kamakoti Peetam had set foot inside the temple.

Thus, after 200 years, the Acharya of Kanchi Kamakoti Peetam was set to step into Chidambaram once again.

Periyava's Entry into Chidambaram Temple

Upon reaching Chidambaram, Periyava set up camp outside the town. A grand reception had been planned for Him by the Dikshitars and devotees. However, early the next morning, Periyava made an unexpected decision.

A Divine Call That Couldn't Be Ignored

- Before dawn, Periyava called one of His attendants and instructed him to accompany Him, carrying only a Madhi cloth (a ritually pure cloth that has been washed, dried, and never touched by others).
- Without informing anyone, Periyava silently walked towards the temple, choosing a time when no devotees would be present.
- He entered through "Thithi Kathavu", an entrance normally used by temple employees before the main doors open for the public.
- Upon entering, He proceeded to the sacred Siva Gangai Teertham (the temple's holy water tank), took a ritualistic snanam (holy bath), changed into fresh Madhi clothes, and adorned Himself with Vibhuti (sacred ash) and Rudraksha beads.

Periyava's Unexpected Presence Stuns the Dikshitars

- Having purified Himself, Periyava walked towards the Kanaka Sabha, where Lord Nataraja is enshrined, and stood in deep meditation before the deity.
- At that moment, the morning pooja was being performed by the temple's chief Dikshitar.
- When the Dikshitar turned around, he was overwhelmed to see Periyava standing there, glowing with an ethereal radiance, appearing no less divine than Lord Shiva Himself.
- The priest was taken aback—Periyava had arrived unannounced, before the grand reception they had planned for Him later in the day.

Periyava's Humble Response

The Dikshitar and other temple priests hurriedly gathered around Maha Periyava, expressing their astonishment.

- Dikshitar: "Periyava! We had arranged a grand welcome for You. We never expected You to arrive like this!"
- Periyava (smiling): "Don't worry. You may still conduct the reception. I shall return again. But upon arriving at Chidambaram, I simply could not wait to have darshan of Lord Nataraja."

Thus, without any formal invitation, rituals, or customs, Periyava shattered a 200-year-old barrier in a single moment, demonstrating that nothing—not even long-standing traditions—could stand between a true seeker and the divine.

The Grand Reception

- As promised, Periyava returned later in the day and graciously accepted the grand welcome arranged for Him.
- The priests, temple authorities, and thousands of devotees celebrated His visit with immense reverence and devotion.
- The long-standing misunderstanding between the Kanchi Peetam and the Chidambaram Dikshitars was thus resolved in a moment of divine grace.

Photo: Periyava picture taken in 1933 at Tanjore

Continuing the Yatra: Periyava's Journey to Porto Novo and Beyond

After His momentous visit to Chidambaram, Periyava continued His journey and reached Parangipettai (Porto Novo), a coastal town in Tamil Nadu.

A Heartfelt Reunion with Bava Maraikayar

- A Muslim businessman named Bava Maraikayar, who owned large Uppalams (salt pans), was an ardent devotee of Periyava.
- He was also the disciple of Periyava's father, Subramanya Sastri, and had known Periyava since He was a small child.
- Seeing Periyava now as a Jagadguru, he was overjoyed and personally led a grand reception with Poorna Kumbham (traditional ceremonial welcome).
- He requested Periyava to bless his salt pans with His divine presence.
- Periyava, respecting his devotion, walked the entire 10-kilometer stretch of the salt pans barefoot, as a gesture of love and acceptance.

Periyava's Northward Yatra Begins

From Porto Novo, Periyava proceeded to Tanjore, where He performed Vyasa Puja and observed Chaturmasyam and Navaratri.

- Here, He reflected that His journey had been ongoing for 14 years, covering numerous Divya Kshetrams (sacred sites).
- With renewed resolve, He decided not to delay His Kasi Yatra any further.

Photo: Periyava picture taken in 1933 at Tanjore Devotee's
Sri T.R. Muthuswamy's House

From Tanjore, Periyava began His long pilgrimage to Kashi, covering hundreds of miles on foot, maintaining His daily spiritual practices, and receiving royal honors from different kingdoms along the way.

Periyava's Divine Yatra Towards Kashi

After completing Navaratri in Tanjore, Maha Periyava made a resolute decision to embark on a pilgrimage to Kashi. His journey was not a casual one; he committed himself to walking at least 20 miles per day, moving steadily towards the sacred city of Kashi. Despite the arduous travel, Periyava never compromised on his daily spiritual rituals, including Chandrasekarendra Pooja and other Vedic observances, maintaining the same discipline and devotion regardless of the hardships of the journey.

This yatra was not a simple walk of an ascetic; it was a grand spiritual procession. Unlike the typical image of a lone saint journeying on foot, Periyava's yatra was an awe-inspiring spectacle—akin to an entire village on the move. His entourage included 200 to 300 people, comprising Vedic scholars, disciples, devotees, cooks, and security personnel, along with cows, elephants, horses, camels, and bullock carts carrying essential supplies. Such was the grandeur of this pilgrimage that it commanded respect from rulers across the land.

During Aurangzeb's reign, a royal decree was issued that no tax should be collected from the Kanchi Kamakoti Acharya's yatra. This tradition continued for centuries, ensuring that Periyava's sacred journey remained unhindered by administrative barriers.

Photo: Periyava picture taken in 1933 at Thiruvidai Maruthur

Periyava's Arrival in Chinna Tippa Samudram (1933 & 1978)

As Periyava journeyed northward from Tanjore, crossing several regions, he reached Chinna Tippa Samudram in 1933. Even today, stone carvings in the region depict Periyava's visit, immortalizing the event for posterity. The significance of his presence was so profound that in 1978, nearly 45 years later, Periyava returned to Chinna Tippa Samudram and chose to stay at the same spot where he had once camped during his earlier yatra.

The people of Chinna Tippa Samudram were overwhelmed with devotional ecstasy at the opportunity to host Periyava once again. His presence was a divine blessing, and they welcomed him with immense reverence, performing elaborate rituals to honor the sage.

Visit to Kadiri – The Land of Lakshmi Narasimha Swamy

From Chinna Tippa Samudram, Periyava continued his yatra to Kadiri, home to the sacred Kadiri Lakshmi Narasimha Swamy Temple, one of the most revered shrines in Anantapur district, Andhra Pradesh.

This ancient temple has deep mythological significance, being associated with Lord Narasimha's incarnation, where Vishnu took on the half-lion, half-man form to slay the demon king Hiranyakashipu. According to legend, after destroying the demon, Lord Narasimha's rage did not subside, and the Devas, along with sages, performed penance to calm him. At this very site, Lord Narasimha is believed to have self-manifested (Swayambhu) from the roots of the Kadiri tree. The name 'Kadiri' itself originates from the Sanskrit word 'Khadri,' meaning the Acacia tree.

Even today, a miraculous phenomenon takes place at this temple— the idol of Lord Narasimha is said to sweat, symbolizing his immense divine energy and eternal presence. This unique occurrence reinforces the belief that the Lord continues to reside in this sacred shrine, protecting and blessing devotees.

Photo: Periyava picture taken in 1934 Srisailam Andra Pradesh

The temple architecture, influenced by the Vijayanagara style, features a majestic Rajagopuram adorned with intricate carvings that depict stories from the Ramayana, Mahabharata, and Vishnu Puranas. Inside the sanctum, the deity Lakshmi Narasimha Swamy, along with Goddess Lakshmi, radiates an aura of divine grace.

Grand festivals such as Brahmotsavam (April-May), Narasimha Jayanti, Vaikunta Ekadasi, and Karthika Deepotsavam draw thousands of devotees each year. It is believed that those who pray here with sincerity are granted courage, protection, and spiritual enlightenment, ultimately leading them towards moksha (liberation).

Periyava's Journey to Srisailam – The Land of Shiva and Shakti

From Kadiri, Periyava continued his sacred pilgrimage, passing through Ananthapur and Dronachalam, before reaching Srisailam, home to the renowned Mallikarjuna Swamy Temple.

The Srisailam Temple is one of the most sacred pilgrimage sites in India, holding immense significance in both Shaivism and Shaktam. This is one of the twelve Jyotirlingas, where Lord Shiva is worshipped as Mallikarjuna Swamy, and also one of the eighteen Maha Shakti Peethas, where Goddess Parvati is venerated as Bhramaramba Devi. This unique distinction makes Srisailam a rare and powerful confluence of both Shiva and Shakti, symbolizing the cosmic balance between Purusha (Shiva) and Prakriti (Shakti).

According to legend, when Kartikeya, the son of Shiva and Parvati, left for Krauncha Mountain in disappointment after Ganesha was chosen as the first deity to be worshipped, Shiva and Parvati came to Srisailam to console him. Their divine presence sanctified the region, and they chose to reside here eternally.

The Krishna River, also known as Patalaganga, flows through this region, and devotees believe that bathing in its sacred waters cleanses one of all sins.

The temple's architecture, built in Vijayanagara and Chalukyan styles, features towering gopurams, intricately carved mandapams, and a sanctum radiating deep spiritual vibrations. Srisailam is also associated with Adi Shankaracharya, who composed the Sivananda Lahari here, and several saints who have performed penance in its holy surroundings.

Pilgrims visiting Srisailam believe that worshipping Mallikarjuna Swamy and Bhramaramba Devi grants moksha (liberation) and absolves them of all karmic bonds. The spiritual energy of Srisailam is unparalleled, making it not just a pilgrimage site, but a center of divine realization, penance, and self-discovery.

Periyava's Journey into Madhya Pradesh – Reaching Ghatwar

After leaving Andhra Pradesh, Periyava entered Madhya Pradesh, reaching the kingdom of Ghatwar. The Queen of Ghatwar, upon hearing about the arrival of the great saint, welcomed Periyava with utmost devotion and reverence. A grand celebration was organized in his honor, and the people of Ghatwar felt blessed to receive his divine presence.

However, Periyava's journey through Madhya Pradesh was not easy. Unlike the plains of the south, the terrains were rugged, and the paths were difficult. The climate posed new challenges, and crossing rivers, forests, and remote regions required immense mental and physical endurance. Yet, Periyava remained undeterred, leading his disciples with the same unwavering faith and divine grace.

As he continued his yatra, Periyava's presence uplifted the spiritual consciousness of the land, leaving behind a trail of blessings, wisdom, and divine vibrations, marking every place he visited as sacred for generations to come.

25

PERIYAVA'S YATRA TO PRAYAG AND KASHI (1934–1935)

Enduring the Scorching Heat in Madhya Pradesh

During His yatra through Madhya Pradesh, the scorching summer heat rose to an unbearable 120 degrees Fahrenheit. Yet, the devoted followers of the Mutt endured these extreme conditions and continued to walk alongside Maha Periyava, unwavering in their commitment.

The terrain of Madhya Pradesh was particularly challenging, with daily distances ranging from 25 to 40 miles. Despite the difficulties, Periyava displayed immense compassion for those carrying the Mena (palanquin). Instead of allowing them to bear the burden, He often chose to walk on foot, giving them relief from carrying the Mena over long distances.

Those who carried Periyava's palanquin experienced something truly divine—an occurrence beyond ordinary comprehension. Years later, a devotee named Bethabogi Kunju narrated an extraordinary incident. He revealed that when Maha Periyava walked by Himself, the Mena became unusually heavy, and the bearers would plead with Him to sit inside. However, the moment He entered, the palanquin felt weightless!

The Divine Mystery of the Mena's Weight

This mystical phenomenon relates to the Ashta Siddhis, the eight supernatural yogic powers described in Hindu scriptures:

- **Anima** – The power to become infinitely small
- **Mahima** – The power to expand infinitely
- **Laghima** – The ability to become weightless
- **Garima** – The ability to become extremely heavy

Maha Periyava, being a realized soul, was beyond the limitations of physical form. When He sat inside the Mena, His divine presence lightened the burden on His devotees, whereas when it was empty, they felt the overwhelming weight of His spiritual energy. This strengthened the faith of His followers, proving that Periyava was not just a saint but an embodiment of supreme spiritual consciousness.

Additionally, Periyava always cared for His devotees' well-being. On particularly hot days, as they walked carrying the palanquin, He would peel fruits such as apples and oranges and offer them to His attendants, ensuring they were nourished.

Arrival at Jabalpur and Bathing in the Sacred Waters (1934)

In 1934, as part of His yatra, Periyava reached Jabalpur, where He bathed in the holy waters along the way. His journey continued toward Prayag, the holiest confluence of rivers.

Periyava at Prayag (Allahabad) – The Sacred Triveni Sangam

On July 23, 1934, Periyava arrived at Prayagai (Allahabad), the revered site of the Triveni Sangam, where the Ganga, Yamuna, and the mystical Saraswati rivers converge. This site has immense spiritual, historical, and mythological significance in Hinduism.

Why Prayag is the Holiest of All Tirthas

- According to **scriptures**, bathing in the **Triveni Sangam** cleanses all sins (**Paapa Vimochana**) and grants **Moksha (liberation)**.
- The site is where **Lord Brahma** performed the **first yajna (sacrificial ritual)** after the creation of the universe, thus earning the name **Prayag** (meaning "place of sacrifice").
- The **Mahabharata** mentions that the **Pandavas** visited this sacred confluence before their final journey.

Importance of Ganga Water from Prayag

When Maha Periyava bathed in the Triveni Sangam, He offered the sand He had carried from Rameshwaram into the holy waters. He also took sacred Ganga Theertam from Prayag.

Taking Ganga water from the Prayag Triveni Sangam holds immense spiritual significance:

1. **Purest Form of Ganga Water** – Prayag is considered **Tirtharaja (King of Pilgrimage Sites)**, making its water the holiest of all.
2. **Spiritual Benefits** – As per the **Padma Purana and Matsya Purana**, Prayag's waters contain the **divine essence of all holy rivers**.
3. **Karma Cleansing & Ancestral Blessings** – The **Garuda Purana** states that offering Prayag Ganga water during **Tarpanam (ancestral rituals)** brings **Pitru Mukti (salvation for ancestors)**.
4. **Used for Worship & Last Rites** – Many Hindu families **store Prayag Ganga water** for **pujas, temple consecrations, and even funeral rites**.
5. **Scientific Healing Properties** – Studies show that Ganga water **contains unique self-purifying properties** due to beneficial minerals.

*Photo: Periyava picture taken in 1934 in Khasi Public
Reception with Maharaj of Khasi.*

Periyava's Darshan at Veni Madhava Temple

After His holy bath, Periyava visited the Veni Madhava Temple, one of the 108 Divya Desams, dedicated to Lord Vishnu. This temple, situated near the Triveni Sangam, is said to be the spiritual guardian of the confluence. It is believed that bathing in the Sangam and worshipping Veni Madhava together ensures complete spiritual purification and Moksha.

Legend has it that even during the Mahabharata era, Lord Krishna instructed the Pandavas to worship Veni Madhava before their exile.

Periyava's Eclipse Bath & Vyasa Puja at Prayag (1934)

In 1934, during His stay in Prayag, a solar eclipse occurred. In keeping with Hindu traditions, Periyava bathed in the Sangam during the eclipse, an act believed to enhance spiritual purification and remove karmic obstacles.

Following this, Periyava conducted the Vyasa Puja, a ritual honoring Sage Vyasa, the revered compiler of the Vedas.

Periyava's Grand Arrival at Kashi (Varanasi) – October 6, 1934

On October 6, 1934, Periyava reached the sacred city of Kashi (Varanasi), one of the oldest living cities in the world. The Kashi Raja and the esteemed Madan Mohan Malaviya of Banaras Hindu University (BHU) led a grand royal welcome for Periyava, with over 10,000 devotees waiting at the Kashi border to receive Him.

Even though the Mutt Manager had earlier worried about whether Kanchi Mutt was well-known in North India, the overwhelming reception in Kashi proved that Periyava's spiritual radiance transcended all boundaries.

Photo: Periyava picture taken in 1934 in Khasi with Maharaj of Khasi.

Periyava's Holy Baths & Worship in Kashi

Periyava took **ritual baths at various ghats**, including:

- **Manikarnika Ghat** – The most sacred cremation ground, where attaining liberation is believed to be guaranteed.
- **Dashashwamedh Ghat** – Known for the famous **Ganga Aarti**.
- **Assi Ghat, Panchganga Ghat**, and others.

He then offered prayers at the Kashi Vishwanath Temple, one of the twelve Jyotirlingas, and worshipped at the Annapoorani, Kalabairavar, Vishalakshi Temples.

Periyava Collects a Sacred Stone from the Sonabhadra River

During His journey, Periyava reached Kail Garh in Uttar Pradesh, where the Sonabhadra River flows. He collected a sacred stone from the river, which had taken the natural form of Lord Ganesha, to be used in Panchayatana Puja.

This act symbolizes Adi Shankaracharya's Smarta tradition, where five deities (Shiva, Vishnu, Devi, Ganesha, and Surya) are worshipped equally as manifestations of Brahman (Supreme Reality).

26

PERIYAVA'S VISIT TO PATNA (PATALIPUTRA) – 1935

When Periyava reached Patna, it coincided with Shankara Jayanti. The King of Patna, Shri Dikari, personally sponsored the grand celebrations.

Here, Sri Babu Rajendra Prasad, along with his family, had the blessed opportunity to have darshan of Maha Periyava. From Patna, Periyava traveled extensively, visiting numerous *samastanams*, temples, and palaces before arriving at Harihar.

Harihar Kshetra: The Sacred Confluence of Shiva and Vishnu

Harihar Kshetra in Bihar is a revered pilgrimage site, particularly famous for the Hariharnath Temple in Sonpur, where Lord Vishnu (*Hari*) and Lord Shiva (*Hara*) are worshipped as one deity. Situated at the confluence of the Ganga and Gandak rivers, this temple holds immense spiritual significance. According to legend, Lord Rama, during his exile, established this temple, making it a sacred site for both Shaivites and Vaishnavites.

The site is also famous for the Sonpur Mela, one of the largest cattle fairs in Asia, historically renowned for its elephant trade. Devotees believe that offering prayers at the temple bestows both material prosperity and spiritual liberation, reinforcing the oneness of two supreme deities.

The Divine Significance of the Gandaki River and Shaligramam

The Gandaki River, also known as the Kantaki River, is deeply revered in Hinduism as it is the only river where Shaligramam stones are naturally found. According to the *Skanda Purana*, Goddess Lakshmi prayed to Lord Vishnu to make his divine form available to devotees for worship. In response, Lord Vishnu manifested as Shaligrama stones in the Gandaki River. These sacred black ammonite fossils bear chakra (disc) markings, symbolizing Vishnu's Sudarshana Chakra.

Taking a Shaligramam from the Gandaki River is considered highly meritorious, and worshipping it is believed to bring divine protection, prosperity, and Moksha (liberation). The river is also closely associated with the Muktinath Temple, a revered pilgrimage site where both Hindus and Buddhists seek salvation. Its waters are believed to purify sins and bestow blessings, making it a key spiritual landmark for Vishnu devotees.

Periyava's Holy Bath in the Gandaki and Journey to Punpun

After taking a holy bath in the sacred waters of the Gandaki River, Periyava continued his journey to Punpun.

The Punpun River, a tributary of the Ganga, holds immense religious significance, particularly in Chhath Puja, an ancient festival dedicated to Surya Bhagavan (Sun God). Thousands of devotees gather on its banks to offer *Arghya* (water oblation) during sunrise and sunset.

The river is mentioned in the *Ramayana*, as it is believed that Mata Sita performed Pind Daan (ancestral offerings) for King Dasharatha on its banks in Falka village, near Punpun town. Because of this, it remains a sacred site for performing Pitru Tarpanam (ancestral rituals). The name Punpun derives from the Sanskrit words *Punya* (virtue) and *Punyam* (sacredness), signifying its purifying nature. Bathing in its waters is believed to cleanse sins and grant spiritual merit.

Periyava's Visit to Gaya: The Land of Salvation

In May 1935, Periyava arrived in Gaya, one of the holiest cities in India, holding immense religious significance in both Hinduism and Buddhism.

According to Hindu tradition, the city derives its name from Gayasura, a powerful demon who, through intense penance, acquired extraordinary spiritual energy. To prevent sinful beings from attaining liberation too easily, the Devas sought Lord Vishnu's intervention. Vishnu, to neutralize Gayasura's power, asked him to lie down and transformed his body into a sacred land where devotees could perform Pind Daan for their ancestors. The Vishnupad Temple, where Lord Vishnu's divine footprint is imprinted, remains the foremost site for these rituals, ensuring Moksha (liberation) for departed souls.

The **Akshaya Vata Vriksha** (also spelled Akshaya Vatam) in **Gaya, Bihar** is a sacred and eternal **banyan tree** believed to be **indestructible** ("Akshaya" means eternal or imperishable). It stands within the **Vishnupad Temple complex**, on the banks of the Phalgu River, and is deeply revered in **Sanatana Dharma**.

According to tradition, it is under this tree that **Lord Vishnu** is said to have granted **moksha (liberation)** to the souls of ancestors. The Akshaya Vata is believed to be a witness to the **Shraddha rituals** performed for **pitrus (departed souls)** and plays a pivotal role in the **Pitru Karyas (ancestral rites)**. Performing **tarpanam or pind daan** under this tree is believed to ensure **eternal blessings and liberation** for one's ancestors.

It is also linked to stories from the **Ramayana** and **Mahabharata**, where **Sri Rama, Sita,** and **Bhishma Pitamaha** are believed to have visited or invoked the sanctity of this place. The tree's immortality is symbolic of the eternal cycle of life, death, and rebirth, and of the divine witness to all karma.

Gaya is also a major Buddhist pilgrimage site, as it is near Bodh Gaya, where Gautama Buddha attained enlightenment under the sacred Bodhi tree. The Falgu River, believed to be the manifestation of celestial rivers Ganga, Yamuna, and Saraswati, enhances its sanctity. Even Mata Sita is said to have performed Pind Daan here, reinforcing its spiritual importance.

Vaitharani River and the Importance of Go-Daanam

Continuing his yatra, Periyava reached Vaitharani, where he performed Go-Daanam (donation of cows).

In Hindu belief, Vaitharani is a divine river that separates the mortal world from the afterlife. The *Garuda Purana* describes it as a fearsome river filled with boiling filth, which sinful souls must wade through as part of their karmic retribution. However, those who have performed righteous deeds and Go-Daanam cross the river with ease, aided by a divine cow.

Photo: Periyava picture taken in 1935 in Calcutta.

Periyava in Bhuvaneshwar and Shankara Jayanti

Periyava then traveled to Bhubaneswar, where he performed the Shankara Jayanti celebrations of that year, honoring Adi Shankaracharya.

Periyava's Visit to Sakshi Gopal

Periyava next visited Sakshi Gopal, a place named after a divine event where Lord Krishna himself became a Sakshi (witness) to uphold justice and truth. The temple here stands as a symbol of Krishna's divine presence and his role as the ultimate witness to truth and devotion.

Periyava's Worship at Puri Jagannath Temple

Finally, Periyava arrived at the **Jagannath Temple in Puri**, one of the most revered temples in India and an essential pilgrimage site in the **Char Dham Yatra**.

Significance of Puri Jagannath Temple

- **Lord Jagannath as the Universal Lord** – The deity's unique form symbolizes the eternal cosmic energy.
- **Mystical Phenomena**:
  - The **temple flag always flies against the wind.**
  - **No bird or aircraft ever flies over the temple.**
  - The **ocean's sound disappears inside the temple premises.**

- **Annual Rath Yatra** – The grand chariot festival where Jagannath, Balabhadra, and Subhadra travel to the **Gundicha Temple**, symbolizing Krishna's journey to Vrindavan.

- **Mahaprasad (Chappan Bhog)** – The sacred offerings cooked in the temple kitchen are believed to be prepared by divine will.
- **Adi Shankaracharya's Govardhan Peetham**, reinforcing **Advaita Vedanta**.

The Jagannath Temple remains a spiritual powerhouse, blending devotion, ancient traditions, and divine mysteries that continue to inspire millions of devotees.

Periyava's yatra through these sacred places exemplifies his profound spiritual mission—reviving ancient traditions, reinforcing dharma, and illuminating the path of righteousness for generations to come.

The Divine Significance of Puri Jagannath Mahaprasadam and Maha Periyava's Reverence

The Mahaprasadam of the Puri Jagannath Temple holds a revered and mystical place in the spiritual traditions of India. More than just sacred food, it is a divine offering deeply woven into the daily rituals of one of the most ancient temples in the country. Prepared in the enormous temple kitchen known as the Rosha Ghara, this Mahaprasadam is unique in its method and sanctity.

The food is cooked in traditional earthen pots, which are stacked vertically—sometimes up to seven tiers—over a wood-fired hearth. In a phenomenon that defies conventional logic, the pot placed at the top gets cooked first, followed by the ones below in sequence. This miraculous occurrence is not scientifically explainable and is revered as a divine mystery, believed to be the will of Lord Jagannath himself.

Every day, over 56 varieties of dishes, known collectively as Chappan Bhog, are prepared by the Suara Sevaks, the traditional cooks of the temple. These sevaks follow strict rituals, preparing the food without tasting or even smelling it, maintaining the sanctity and discipline passed down through generations. Once cooked, the offerings are first made to Lord Jagannath, Balabhadra, and Subhadra. Only after this divine offering is the food distributed to the devotees as Mahaprasadam, believed to carry immense spiritual power and the ability to purify one's soul.

Maha Periyava and the Sacred Mahaprasadam

During his stay at Kanchipuram, the renowned Justice Ranganath Mishra, a devout follower of Maha Periyava, once came to seek His blessings. During their conversation, Periyava spoke at length about the sanctity and divine nature of the Mahaprasadam from Puri. He expressed his desire to receive the holy offering. In his next visit, Justice Mishra took a flight to Puri, obtained the Mahaprasadam, and returned to present it to Periyava.

What makes this incident especially remarkable is that Maha Periyava was known never to consume food prepared by anyone other than the Sevarthis (servitors) of the Kanchi Mutt. However, in this rare instance, He made an exception and partook of the Mahaprasadam, stating that "Wherever the sacred prasadam of Puri Jagannath is available, in whatever form, we must never hesitate to accept it." This incident reflects not only the spiritual significance of the Mahaprasadam but also Periyava's universal respect for all sacred traditions within Sanatana Dharma.

Puri – The Eastern Dham and Confluence of Traditions

Earlier in this narrative, we discussed the Char Dham, the four cardinal abodes of Lord Vishnu as established by Adi Shankaracharya—

Badrinath in the north, Rameswaram in the south, Dwarka in the west, and Puri in the east. Among these, Puri stands out uniquely, not just as a Vishnu shrine but as a center where the Vaishnavite and Shakta traditions meet.

This is because the Vimala Peetam, a powerful Shakti Peetam, resides within the Puri Jagannath temple complex. As per belief, the navel (nabhi) of Sati Devi fell at this very spot, sanctifying it. The Vimala Devi shrine was consecrated by Adi Shankaracharya during his travels, marking Puri as both a Vishnu and Shakti Kshetra. Importantly, the offerings to Lord Jagannath are considered complete only after they are offered to Goddess Vimala, underscoring her supreme spiritual position.

This unique spiritual synthesis highlights the unity of Shaiva, Vaishnava, and Shakta traditions, a vision deeply emphasized by Adi Shankara throughout his teachings and travels.

Maha Periyava's Visit to Puri and Beyond

When Maha Periyava visited Puri, he was received with great honor by the Maharaja of Puri. A ceremonial welcome was held in the sacred Mukthi Mandapa Sabha, the very spot where Adi Shankaracharya is believed to have meditated. The Vidvans of the Sabha humbly requested Periyava to ascend the Peetam once occupied by Adi Shankara and bless everyone present.

Periyava sat on the Peetam and delivered an Upanyasam (spiritual discourse) from there—an event of immense spiritual significance. He later had darshan at the Jagannath temple and took a holy dip in the ocean, which is part of the traditional pilgrimage to Puri.

Following this, Periyava continued His journey to Chilka Lake, India's largest coastal lagoon and the second-largest in the world.

The lake is not only ecologically vital but also spiritually important. Kalijai Temple, situated on an island in the lake, is dedicated to Goddess Kalijai, believed to be an incarnation of Goddess Kali. Chilka thus combines the serene beauty of nature with deep spiritual resonance.

27

PERIYAVA'S YATRA BACK TO KUMBAKONAM (1936–1939)

The Return Journey: A Divine Continuum of Tapasya and Grace

After the spiritually momentous visit to Jagannath Puri, where Maha Periyava took part in profound religious observances and paid respects at the sacred Vimala Shakti Peetam and the Jagannath Temple, He began the southern return leg of His 21-year-long Kashi Yatra. This final stretch of the journey, undertaken from 1936 to 1939, is no less significant—it carried the echoes of deep tapas, divine interactions, meticulous observance of scriptural mandates, and unwavering commitment to the spiritual upliftment of Bharat.

Periyava's Journey Across Andhra Pradesh: A Tapestry of Temples and Tapas

From Puri, Periyava entered present-day Andhra Pradesh, arriving in Brahmapur (Berhampur) in 1936. There, He observed the Chaturmasya Vratham—a sacred vow of spiritual austerity undertaken during the four-month rainy season, when Sannyasis stay in one place to engage in intense spiritual practices, scriptural discourses, and guiding devotees.

The Sacred Pilgrimage Continues

From Brahmapur, Periyava's journey carried Him to Srikurmam, one of the few temples where Lord Vishnu is worshiped in Kurma (tortoise) avatar. This temple, located near Srikakulam, is revered as an ancient shrine mentioned even in the Skanda Purana. Periyava's darshan at this rare Kshetra showed His commitment to visiting even lesser-known yet spiritually potent sites of the Sanatana Dharma tradition.

Following Srikurmam, He visited Vizianagaram, where He performed the Navaratri Pooja, invoking the Divine Mother during the most auspicious nine nights of Devi worship. This was not just a pooja but a profound reaffirmation of the Shakta tradition within the inclusive Vedantic framework of Periyava's journey.

Next, He traveled to Simhachalam, the sacred abode of Sri Varaha Lakshmi Narasimha Swamy, a temple that fuses the fierce Narasimha and Varaha avatars of Vishnu. The Lord here is always covered in sandalwood paste, and only once a year—on Akshaya Tritiya—is the original murti visible. Periyava's darshan here was marked by divine stillness, and many devotees witnessed His radiance reflecting the glory of the Lord.

From there, Periyava moved on to Visakhapatnam, touching the shores of the Bay of Bengal once more, before continuing deeper into the heartland of Andhra Pradesh.

1937: The Year of Deepened Observance and Scholarly Engagement

In 1937, Periyava reached Kakinada, where His presence drew large crowds and fostered an atmosphere of Vedic learning and devotion. From there, He proceeded to Palakollu, a sacred town near Narsapur, known for its historical Shiva temple—Ksheera

Ramalingeswara Swamy, one of the five Pancharama Kshetras of Andhra.

It was here that Periyava observed the Vyasa Puja and once again performed the Chaturmasya Vratham. During this time, He delivered discourses on the Vedas, Smritis, and Dharma Shastras, attracting pandits and aspirants from across the Telugu-speaking regions. His humility and depth of knowledge impressed even the most erudite scholars.

The Ekadashi Observance at Hukumpet: A Lesson in Scriptural Precision

From Palakollu, Periyava traveled to Hukumpet, a quiet village where He performed the Navaratri Pooja that year. As the Mutt was preparing to depart the next morning, Periyava gently intervened, reminding the team,

"Tomorrow is Ekadashi. A Sannyasi must not leave a place during Ekadasi with an empty stomach. It is not auspicious for the village."

This statement was profound. It showed that even the timing of a Sannyasi's departure was tied to the welfare of the place and its people. Ekadashi is a sacred tithi, and the presence of a Tapasvi like Periyava during such a day was considered highly auspicious. His adherence to Dharma was not merely personal—He ensured that His actions upheld cosmic order and brought collective spiritual benefit.

Godavari Darshan and Visit to Kanaka Durga Temple

From Hukumpet, Periyava traveled to Polavaram and then to Rajahmundry, one of the most ancient and culturally rich towns on the banks of the sacred Godavari River—the Dakshina Ganga. Periyava took a holy dip in the Godavari, as is customary for pilgrims, and the town reverberated with Vedic chants and devotional hymns during His stay.

He then moved to Vijayawada, Took holy dip in Krishna river where He offered his respects at the Kanaka Durga Temple, seated majestically atop Indrakeeladri Hill. The Goddess here is believed to have manifested herself for Arjuna's penance, blessing him with the Pasupatastra. Periyava's worship at this Shakti Peetam symbolized the deep reverence He had for all facets of the Divine Mother—Durga, Kali, and Shakti in Her various manifestations.

The Miraculous Temple of Mangalagiri

Next, Periyava visited the mystical shrine of Panakala Lakshmi Narasimha Swamy at Mangalagiri. Here, the Lord is offered only Panakam (jaggery water). The divine mystery of the temple is that only half of the offered Panakam is consumed by the deity, while the rest flows back—a visible miracle witnessed by generations. This reflects the living presence of the Lord and the spiritual magnetism of the site.

Periyava stood in awe before the Lord, offering His prayers in silent reverence. Devotees accompanying Him recalled how even nature seemed to quiet itself when He stood in front of the deity, as if recognizing the union of tapas and bhakti.

Guntur: A Beacon of Vedic Wisdom and Scholarly Glory

In 1938, Periyava reached Guntur, where He arranged a grand Vidwat Sadas, inviting Vedic scholars, Shastris, and grammarians from across the Telugu and Tamil regions. It was here that Umamaheswara Sastrigal, a distinguished scholar and devotee, composed 170 Sanskrit slokas in praise of Periyava, and recited them before the audience. Periyava, with utmost humility, blessed the scholar and emphasized that all praises should go to Sanatana Dharma and the Guru Parampara.

Such gatherings weren't mere ceremonies. They revived the oral tradition of knowledge, challenged scholars to deepen their understanding, and reaffirmed the centrality of the Vedas in India's spiritual life.

This was not the first time such profound tributes were paid. We recall the Muslim scholar from Salem and the Sringeri Mutt manager at Kashi, who had earlier composed extensive stotras in Sanskrit to honor Periyava, reflecting the universality of His appeal across communities and traditions.

Photo: Periyava picture taken in 1938 in Guntur

Unparalleled Memory and Divine Grace

Throughout this long journey, Periyava's memory left people in awe. He would call out devotees by name—even those He had met decades ago—recalling not only their names but details about their families, homes, and prior interactions. This wasn't mere memory— it was divya drishti, the divine sight that flows from deep tapasya and communion with the Supreme.

Photo: Periyava picture taken in 1939 Andra

Photo: Periyava picture taken in 1939 in Nellore

The Culmination: Return via Sacred Southern Shrines

From Guntur, Periyava's divine journey continued through Nellore, Tirupati, Tirutani, Kanchipuram, Villupuram, and Thiruvarur—each place receiving His grace and spiritual benediction. He offered prayers at these ancient Kshetras, re-establishing the dharmic vibrations at each stop.

Finally, on 10th June 1939, Periyava reached Rameswaram, the traditional end-point of a Kashi Yatra. In accordance with tradition, He performed Abhishekam to Lord Ramanatha Swamy with Ganga Theertham, carried from Kashi, and chanted Ekadasa Rudram, concluding the sacred yatra.

On 29th June 1939, after 21 years of divine wandering, intense tapas, spiritual teachings, and rejuvenation of Dharma across Bharat, Periyava returned to the Kumbakonam Mutt.

The Legacy of the Kashi Yatra

This Kashi Yatra of Maha Periyava (1919–1939) stands unparalleled—not just in terms of duration, but in its depth, intent, and spiritual magnitude. No other spiritual master in recent history has undertaken such a Pan-Bharat Yatra, visiting every important Tirtha, reviving ancient temples, strengthening the bonds of Dharma, and uniting all traditions—Shaiva, Vaishnava, Shakta, Smartha—under the grand umbrella of Sanatana Dharma.

It is said that merely listening to or reading the story of this yatra confers the merit of undertaking the pilgrimage oneself. The divine footsteps of Periyava have not only sanctified the land but have planted the seeds of spiritual revival that continue to sprout even today.

This was no ordinary journey—it was Yatra as Yajna, a pilgrimage as penance, and a walk of wisdom across the sacred geography of Bharatavarsha.

ॐ

28

CONCLUSION: THE DAWN OF A TIMELESS LIGHT

As this volume draws to a close, retracing the sacred life of Jagadguru Sri Chandrasekarendra Saraswati Sankaracharya Swamigal—Maha Periyava—from his divine birth in 1894 to the culmination of his Kashi Yatra in 1939, we find ourselves humbled before the monumental spiritual journey of a soul born to uplift dharma, rekindle Vedic wisdom, and embody the very spirit of Sanatana Dharma in its purest form.

This is not just a historical biography—it is a yatra in itself. A spiritual pilgrimage through time, events, and divine encounters that reflect the grace, simplicity, and transcendental vision of Maha Periyava.

Let us now recapitulate and reflect upon this sacred journey.

Birth of a Divine Being (1894)

In the quiet town of Villupuram in Tamil Nadu, in the year 1894, a child was born who would go on to transform the spiritual landscape of modern India. Swaminathan—later known as Sri Chandrasekarendra Saraswati—was born into a pious Housala Smartha Brahmin family, under auspicious circumstances that marked his birth as extraordinary. From his early years, he displayed an unusual serenity, intellectual brilliance, and an innate spiritual gravitas.

His childhood was marked by extraordinary memory, sharpness of intellect, and a natural affinity toward Vedic learning. Though his formal education followed the usual path, the deeper stirrings of his soul were preparing him for a destiny far beyond the worldly life.

Divine Ascension to the Peetam (1907)

At the age of 13, destiny revealed its design. With the untimely demise of the 66th Acharya of the Kanchi Kamakoti Peetam, and the 67th Acharya, young Swaminathan was ordained as the 68th Shankaracharya of the Peetam in 1907. The transformation from a boy to a Jagadguru was swift yet divinely orchestrated. Renamed Sri Chandrasekarendra Saraswati, the young Acharya took on the enormous responsibility of guiding the spiritual, moral, and cultural fabric of the land.

Despite his tender age, Maha Periyava's innate wisdom, humility, and sense of purpose astounded all. Scholars bowed before his knowledge. Devotees were drawn by his compassion. Even kings and administrators revered him as a living embodiment of dharma.

The Early Years at the Peetam (1907–1919)

The initial years of Maha Periyava's tenure as the Peetadhipathi were spent deepening his understanding of the vast traditions, scriptures, and dharmic responsibilities entrusted to him. He did not rush into outward actions. Instead, he introspected, studied, and aligned himself with the spiritual legacy of Adi Shankaracharya. Under his guidance, the Peetam grew in stature—not in riches, but in moral and spiritual authority.

He exhibited a rare blend of Advaitic detachment and day-to-day attention to detail. His guidance was practical, his discourses simple, and his wisdom profound. Every word he spoke carried the vibration of truth. Every act he performed upheld dharma.

His early discourses stressed the importance of Vedic education, the role of the Brahmana as a torchbearer of dharma, and the vital necessity of preserving India's spiritual heritage amid colonial and modernist influences.

The Great Kashi Yatra (1919–1939)

In 1919, Maha Periyava set out on what would become one of the most extraordinary spiritual journeys in recorded history—a 21-year long *padayatra* across the sacred landscape of Bharat. His purpose was manifold: to awaken dharma, revive Vedic traditions, unite diverse regions in spiritual harmony, and bless the masses with his presence.

Starting from Kumbakonam, the yatra took him through villages, towns, forests, and pilgrim centers. Unlike conventional travels, this was not a tour—it was tapasya on foot. With no comfort, no urgency, and no ego, he walked with the grace of a rishi and the humility of a sadhu.

Every halt was a divine encounter. Temples were revitalized. Vedic scholars were honored. Forgotten customs were restored. Conversations with villagers, officials, and scholars helped forge a deeper connection between the Mutt and the people. In every village, a festival of faith unfolded.

His travels through the Tamil regions, Karnataka, and Kerala were marked by intense spiritual activities: from Chaturmasya Vrathams to Vidwat Sadas, from temple renovations to installation of discipline in Vedic pathshalas.

Uplifting the Marginalized

Maha Periyava's compassion was not limited to the learned elite. He walked into the huts of the poor, sat beside Harijans, shared his alms with the hungry, and spoke to children with the love of a grandfather. In an age when social divisions ran deep, he stood tall as a unifying force.

In one of the defining moments, a Muslim scholar in Salem composed Sanskrit verses in his praise. In Kashi, even the Sringeri Mutt Manager offered hundreds of slokas in adoration. Such universal reverence is rare—even among saints—and speaks to the divine magnetism of Periyava's presence.

The Spiritual Zenith: Kashi and Beyond

Reaching Kashi, the spiritual capital of India, was not merely a milestone in distance but the zenith of his inner yatra. Maha Periyava performed sacred rituals, interacted with scholars from all traditions, and offered worship at the holiest of sites. The Ganga bowed to receive him. The traditions of Bharat stood rejuvenated in his presence.

From Kashi, the Yatra extended further north and east to Prayagraj, Gaya, Puri, and deep into Andhra Pradesh and Tamil Nadu. Every step was marked by spiritual events: Vyasa Pujas, Chaturmasya Vratas, Navaratri Poojas, and more. At Palakollu, his teaching on the Ekadashi Vrata showed his precise adherence to Shastric injunctions—even in matters unnoticed by others.

His worship at the sacred Kanaka Durga Temple in Vijayawada, Mangala Giri's Panakala Lakshmi Narasimha, and Vidwat Sadas in Guntur—all were divine chapters in a sacred epic.

The Return: Full Circle at Rameswaram (1939)

After touching the heart of India and awakening countless lives, Maha Periyava finally reached Rameswaram in June 1939. There, he offered the concluding rituals of the Kashi Yatra: Abhishekam to Sri

Ramanatha Swamy with Ganga Theertham and chanting of Ekadasa Rudram. This symbolic act marked not just the physical completion of a 21-year journey, but the spiritual consummation of a grand yagna that had uplifted an entire nation.

On 29th June 1939, he returned to Kumbakonam Mutt—a home coming that echoed through the hearts of thousands. The boy who had left as a young Acharya returned as a towering spiritual giant.

The Legacy of the Yatra

This Kashi Yatra was no ordinary pilgrimage. It was a manifestation of divinely ordained purpose—uniting temples, minds, and hearts under the banner of Advaita and dharma. No other spiritual leader in modern India undertook such a massive journey on foot, for such an extended period, with such humility and grace.

The journey established Maha Periyava as a Jagadguru in the truest sense—not just in title, but in impact. He was a guide to the world, a beacon of timeless wisdom, and a living bridge between ancient traditions and a changing world.

Unfailing Memory, Unmatched Humility

Throughout this divine journey, Maha Periyava exhibited traits that astonished even the most skeptical. His unfailing memory allowed him to recall names, family histories, and even minor conversations with devotees across years and geographies. Yet he never claimed greatness.

His humility was not an affectation—it was his nature. He preferred to sleep on the floor, eat with minimal needs, and travel barefoot. Even when offered royal treatment by kings or administrators, he remained indifferent—grounded in his realization of the Self.

The Man Who Carried the Vedas

By the time the Kashi Yatra concluded, Maha Periyava had not only carried the flag of the Kanchi Kamakoti Peetam across Bharat but had also reawakened the soul of India. He carried the Vedas in his being—not as a scripture, but as lived experience. His very presence radiated the essence of Upanishadic silence, Bhagavad Gita's wisdom, and Shankara's clarity.

A Life Beyond Time

The period from 1894 to 1939 may be seen as a chronological window, but in truth, it covers an eternal saga. From the divine spark of his birth to the blazing flame of his yatra, Maha Periyava's life is a scripture in motion. Every incident, every word, every step is a teaching for posterity.

He did not seek followers. He did not establish a new cult. He did not crave fame or power. He simply *was*—a true renunciate, a dharmic monarch, a silent prophet of Sanatana Dharma in 20th century itself.

29

THIS BOOK: A HUMBLE OFFERING

This book has attempted to follow the sacred footprints of Maha Periyava across the landscapes of Bharat and the hearts of its people. It is but a glimpse—a humble attempt to capture the fragrance of an ageless flower.

For devotees, this book is a pilgrimage. For seekers, it is a guide. For the curious, it is an inspiration. And for those who walk the path of dharma, it is a reminder that saints still walk among us—and their lives continue to uplift us even decades after they leave the physical plane.

30

THE JOURNEY AHEAD

Though this book ends here, Maha Periyava's journey did not. After 1939, he would go on to shape the spiritual destiny of India for several more decades, mentoring generations, influencing social policies, and living as a perfect jivanmukta—a realized soul who walked the earth with compassion and silence.

That story belongs to the next volume.

For now, we bow in reverence.

To the Guru.

To the Yatra.

To the Light that never fades.

Jaya Jaya Shankara! Hara Hara Shankara!

ॐ

Glossary (A to Z)

A

- ### Acharya (आचार्य)

  Meaning: A spiritual teacher or preceptor, especially one who imparts knowledge of the scriptures.

  Significance: Maha Periyava, as the 68th Acharya of the Kanchi Kamakoti Peetham, upheld the Guru-Shishya parampara and guided the Mutt and devotees with spiritual wisdom.

- ### Adi Shankaracharya (आदि शङ्कराचार्य)

  Meaning: A philosopher and theologian who consolidated the doctrine of Advaita Vedanta.

  Significance: Considered the spiritual ancestor of the Kanchi Kamakoti Peetham; Maha Periyava was seen as a direct spiritual descendant upholding the same Vedic tradition.

- ### Abhishekam (अभिषेकम्)

  Meaning: Ritual bathing of a deity's idol with sacred substances such as milk, honey, or water.

  Significance: Periyava performed Abhishekam at many temples, including Rameswaram and Kasi, emphasizing the importance of sacred worship.

- **Agnihotra (अग्निहोत्र)**

  Meaning: A Vedic fire ritual performed to purify the environment and self.

  Significance: Symbol of adherence to Vedic rituals, often emphasized by Periyava in his discourses.

B

- **Bhiksha (भिक्षा)**

  Meaning: Alms received by a sannyasi (renunciate) as part of spiritual practice.

  Significance: Periyava, during his yatra, received bhiksha from humble devotees, reinforcing humility and spiritual discipline.

- **Bhakti (भक्ति)**

  Meaning: Devotion or loving worship towards the Divine.

  Significance: Central to Periyava's teachings; he inspired bhakti across caste, creed, and community.

C

- **Chaturmasya Vratham (चातुर्मास्य व्रतम्)**

  Meaning: A four-month vow observed by ascetics during the monsoon season.

  Significance: Periyava observed this rigorously, conducting discourses and Vedic rituals during the period.

D

- **Darshan (दर्शनम्)**

  Meaning: Sight or audience with a deity or enlightened soul.

  Significance: Thousands sought Periyava's darshan for spiritual upliftment and blessings.

- **Dharmic (धार्मिक)**

  Meaning: Pertaining to Dharma; righteous conduct.
  Significance: Every action of Periyava was rooted in Dharmic values.

E

- **Ekadashi (एकादशी)**

  Meaning: The eleventh day of the lunar fortnight, sacred for fasting and prayer.
  Significance: Periyava followed Ekadashi Vrata with great strictness, teaching the importance of discipline.

G

- **Ganga Theertham (गङ्गा तीर्थम्)**

  Meaning: Holy water from the Ganga River.
  Significance: Used by Periyava for rituals, especially during the Rameswaram abhishekam.

- **Guru Parampara (गुरु परम्परा)**

  Meaning: The unbroken lineage of spiritual teachers.
  Significance: Periyava is part of this ancient lineage tracing back to Adi Shankaracharya.

H

- **Homa (होम)**

  Meaning: A Vedic fire offering ritual.
  Significance: Performed during important occasions.

J

- **Jagadguru (जगद्गुरु)**

  Meaning: 'Guru of the Universe'; a title given to supreme spiritual masters.

Significance: Maha Periyava was revered as Jagadguru by all sects of Hindu society.

- ## Japa (जप)

  Meaning: Repetition of a divine name or mantra.
  Significance: Practiced and recommended by Periyava for spiritual progress.

K

- ## Kumbabhishekam (कुम्भाभिषेकम्)

  Meaning: A consecration ritual performed in temples.
  Significance: Periyava participated in many such rituals across India.

- ## Kashi Yatra (काशी यात्रा)

  Meaning: A pilgrimage to Kashi (Varanasi), the sacred city on the banks of the Ganga.
  Significance: Periyava's 21-year yatra is unmatched in spiritual depth and scope.

M

- ## Matha/Mutt (मठ)

  Meaning: A monastic institution or spiritual center.
  Significance: The Kanchi Kamakoti Mutt served as the seat of Periyava's spiritual authority.

- ## Mangala Giri (मङ्गलगिरि)

  Meaning: A sacred hill in Andhra Pradesh with a unique Narasimha temple.
  Significance: Periyava's visit highlighted his reverence for regional deities.

- **Moksha (मोक्ष)**

  Meaning: Liberation from the cycle of birth and death.

  Significance: Ultimate goal of life, as emphasized by Periyava's teachings.

N

- **Navaratri (नवरात्रि)**

  Meaning: A nine-night festival dedicated to the Divine Mother.

  Significance: Periyava performed intense poojas and discourses during Navaratri.

P

- **Panakam (पानकम्)**

  Meaning: A sweet drink offered to deities, made with jaggery and water.

  Significance: Offered at the Narasimha temple in Mangala Giri visited by Periyava.

- **Punya (पुण्य)**

  Meaning: Spiritual merit earned through righteous actions.

  Significance: Reading about Periyava's life is believed to confer punya.

R

- **Rudram (रुद्रम्)**

  Meaning: A powerful Vedic hymn dedicated to Lord Shiva.

  Significance: Chanted during the abhishekam by Periyava, symbolizing the end of the Kashi Yatra.

- **Rishi (ऋषि)**

  Meaning: A seer or sage who has realized spiritual truths.
  Significance: Periyava is often referred to as a modern-day Rishi.

S

- **Sannyasa (संन्यास)**

  Meaning: The renounced stage of life dedicated to spiritual pursuits.
  Significance: Periyava embraced sannyasa at a young age, dedicating his life to Dharma.

- **Shakti Peetham (शक्ति पीठम्)**

  Meaning: Sacred abodes of the Divine Mother.
  Significance: Periyava visited many such as Kamakshi (Kanchipuram) and Kanaka Durga (Vijayawada).

- **Srikurmam (श्रीकूर्मम्)**

  Meaning: An ancient temple dedicated to the Kurma (tortoise) avatar of Vishnu.
  Significance: A rare and spiritually potent site visited by Periyava.

T

- **Tapas (तपस्)**

  Meaning: Austerity or penance.
  Significance: Periyava's life was one of intense tapas, reflected in his simple lifestyle and spiritual vigor.

- **Theertham (तीर्थम्)**

  Meaning: Sacred water or pilgrimage place.
  Significance: Integral to rituals and symbolic of purity.

U

- **Upanishads (उपनिषद्)**

  Meaning: Ancient spiritual texts revealing ultimate truths of existence.

  Significance: Periyava often quoted Upanishadic wisdom in his discourses.

V

- **Veda (वेद)**

  Meaning: The most ancient and sacred scriptures of Hinduism.

  Significance: Periyava devoted his life to the protection and propagation of Vedic Dharma.

- **Vidwat Sadas (विद्वत्सदस्)**

  Meaning: A gathering of learned scholars for spiritual and scriptural debate.

  Significance: Periyava organized several.

- **Vijayanagaram (विजयनगरम्)**

  Meaning: A historical region in Andhra Pradesh.

  Significance: Site of one of Periyava's Navaratri poojas.

Y

- **Yatra (यात्रा)**

  Meaning: A pilgrimage or spiritual journey.

  Significance: Periyava's Kashi Yatra is one of the most remarkable in Indian spiritual history.

- **Yajna (यज्ञ)**

  Meaning: A Vedic ritual involving offerings into a sacred fire.

  Significance: Symbol of self-sacrifice and dharmic living.

9 798889 293528